A Dictionary
of Quotes
From the
Saints

A Dictionary of Quotes From the Saints

PAUL THIGPEN

CHARIS

SERVANT PUBLICATIONS
ANN ARBOR, MICHIGAN

Charis Books is an imprint of Servant Publications especially designed to serve Roman Catholics.

Published by Servant Publications
P.O. Box 8617
Ann Arbor, Michigan 48107

Cover design: Eric Walljasper

01 02 03 04 10 9 8 7 6 5 4 3 2 1

Printed in the United States of America
ISBN 0-56955-193-6

LIBRARY OF CONGRESS CATALOGING-IN-PUBLICATION DATA

A dictionary of quotes from the saints / [compiled by] Paul Thigpen.
    p. cm.
  ISBN 1-56955-193-6 (alk. paper)
  1. Christian life–Quotations, maxims, etc. 2. Christian life–Catholic authors. 3. Christian saints–
Quotations. 4. Quotations, English. I. Thigpen, Thomas Paul, 1954-

BX2350.2 .D496 2000
282–dc21   00-052352

For my dear friend Scott,
who, like St. Miguel of Ecuador,
is quite happy with only
a "room, some books, and a nearby chapel."

INTRODUCTION

Abba Theodore, a respected abbot among the monks in the deserts of ancient Egypt, once criticized a younger monk as someone who collected the wise sayings of others in order to "retail" them. The abbot's words challenged me as I began to compile this collection: Was I simply "marketing" the saints' wisdom for my own purposes?

Then I reread the account of Abba Theodore's remark and took comfort in the context of his complaint. The other monk, the abbot was noting, concealed the sources of his borrowed sayings and took credit for them himself. This collection, on the other hand, gladly notes the sources, because it is the holy integrity of the saints' lives that lends such weight to their words and urges us to ponder carefully what they have to tell us.

At the same time, a study of the saints' lives shows that few of them would or even could take credit themselves for the insights recorded here. From their perspective, originality is not the goal, but rather faithfulness to a tradition: They aim, not to be novel, but to echo authentically the life and wisdom of Christ as these are expressed in a variety of concrete historical circumstances. The striking parallels between quotes from saints who lived in drastically different conditions of time, place, and culture only confirm the repeated insistence of these men and women that truth is one, that wisdom is ancient, that the human condition is universal, and that the way to God is narrow.

Space constraints forced the omission of countless quite similar quotes that would have reflected this reality even more clearly. Instead, I have had to offer a sampling that suggests the "consensus of the saints" across the centuries and around the globe. Quotes are arranged in rough chronological order under each heading as a way of reflecting historical continuity and development.

In the choice of subjects, I tried to include the topics that are fundamental to Christian faith and experience; but the whimsical and even the comical appear here as well—lest we presume that the saints were humorless. Some topics on which the saints often focused, which are nevertheless ignored by our contemporaries, receive considerable attention here as a way of allowing them to rebuke us for our neglect. The result, I trust, is a collection of thoughts that will inspire and provoke, puzzle and comfort, startle and enlighten.

A list of the sources with brief biographical identifiers appears at the end in alphabetical order by first name. This list includes the titles ascribed to these saintly men and women according to their current place in the process of formal canonization—that is, the process by which the Catholic Church comes to recognize officially and publicly that a person has entered into eternal glory in heaven.

When an interested party or group approaches a bishop to advocate that a certain (deceased) candidate be canonized, and the bishop submits a report on that individual to the Congregation for the Causes of Saints, the candidate is first deemed "Servant of God." Once the Congregation verifies that the candidate practiced virtue to a heroic degree or died a martyr's death, and recommends the cause, if the Holy Father accepts the report the candidate is called "Venerable." Next, the process of beatification occurs when miracles associated with the candidate during life or after death have been studied and confirmed; the candidate is then called "Blessed." Finally, the process is complete when the Church fully canonizes the candidate and ascribes the title "Saint," recommending the person to the universal Church for veneration, imitation, and petition.

Veneration, imitation, and petition: in brief, these are the reasons for producing a dictionary of quotes from the saints, so that the reader can honor them by imitating them and asking their assistance in doing so. My desire is to help you enter more fully into the glorious communion of saints by acquainting you more deeply with these elder brothers and sisters in Christ, to draw you closer to them as friends so that they might draw you closer into their own friendship with God.

Pope St. Clement I said it best: "Follow the saints—because those who follow them will themselves become saints."

Paul Thigpen

ABANDONMENT OF SELF TO GOD

Abandon yourself utterly for the love of God, and in this way you will become truly happy.

Henry Suso

Lose yourself wholly; and the more you lose, the more you will find.

Catherine of Siena

Let each one remember that he will make progress in all spiritual things only insofar as he rids himself of self-love, self-will, and self-interest.

Ignatius Loyola

I need nothing but God, and to lose myself in the heart of God.

Margaret Mary Alacoque

Let us throw ourselves into the ocean of His goodness, where every failing will be canceled and anxiety turned into love.

Paul of the Cross

I wish I could lose myself and never find myself except in God!

John Vianney

ABORTION

A woman who deliberately destroys a fetus is answerable for murder. And any fine distinction between its being completely formed or unformed is not admissible among us.

Basil the Great

ADVENT

There are three distinct comings of the Lord of which I know: His coming to men, His coming into men, and His coming against men.

Bernard of Clairvaux

AFFECTIONS

We don't walk to God with the feet of our body, nor would wings, if we had them, carry us to Him; but we go to Him by the affections of our soul.

Augustine of Hippo

AFFLICTION — *See also Sorrow; Trials*

Let your afflictions be books to admonish you.

Ephraem the Syrian

God measures out affliction according to our need.

John Chrysostom

One and the same violence of affliction proves, purifies, and melts the good, and condemns, wastes, and casts out the bad.

Augustine of Hippo

You who teach us by sorrow, and wound us in order to heal us, and kill us so that we may not die apart from You.

Augustine of Hippo

Why are we sad? Why do we blame God? Evils abound in the world so that the world will fail to seduce us into loving it.

Augustine of Hippo

The more we are afflicted in this world, the greater is our assurance in the next; the more we sorrow in the present, the greater will be our joy in the future.

Isidore of Seville

If things always went wrong, no one could endure it; if things always went well, everyone would become arrogant.

Bernard of Clairvaux

Tribulation is a gift from God—one that He especially gives His special friends.

Thomas More

Without the burden of afflictions it is impossible to reach the height of grace. The gift of grace increases as the struggles increase.

Rose of Lima

Whenever anything disagreeable or displeasing happens to you, remember Christ crucified and be silent.

John of the Cross

See to it that you're not suddenly saddened by the adversities of this world, for you don't know the good they bring, being ordained in the judgments of God for the everlasting joy of the elect.

John of the Cross

Many would be willing to have afflictions provided that they be not inconvenienced by them.

Francis de Sales

It is not enough to be afflicted because God wills it; but we must be so as He wills it, when He wills it, for as long as He wills it, and exactly in the manner in which it pleases Him.

Francis de Sales

Should we not adore God's will in profound submission, and lovingly kiss the rod with which He reproves His elect?

Jane Frances de Chantal

AGE, AGING

When men wish for old age for themselves, what else do they wish for but lengthened infirmity?

Augustine of Hippo

Let your old age be childlike, and your childhood like old age; that is, so that neither may your wisdom be with pride, nor your humility without wisdom.

Augustine of Hippo

ALMSGIVING

Our prayers become effective through almsgiving; life is redeemed from dangers by almsgiving; souls are delivered from death by almsgiving.

Cyprian of Carthage

The bread you store up belongs to the hungry; the cloak that lies in your chest belongs to the naked; the gold you have hidden in the ground belongs to the poor.

Basil the Great

Scatter what you have, then, so that you may not lose; give away, so that you may keep; lay out, so that you may save; spend, so that you may gain. If your treasures are to be hoarded, don't be the one who hoards them, for in doing so you will surely be throwing them away. Instead, entrust them to God, for no one can steal them from Him.... Lend to Him who gives an interest greater than the principal.

John Chrysostom

The rich man who gives to the poor does not bestow alms but pays a debt.

Ambrose of Milan

If we can enter the church day and night and implore God to hear our prayers, how careful we should be to hear and grant the petitions of our neighbors in need.

Francis of Assisi

We must be charitable and humble and give alms, because they wash the stains of sin from our souls.

Francis of Assisi

It would be considered a theft on our part if we didn't give to someone in greater need than we are.

Francis of Assisi

We must give alms. Charity wins souls and draws them to virtue.

Angela Merici

AMBITION

The only true riches are those that make us rich in virtue. Therefore, if you want to be rich, beloved, love true riches. If you aspire to the heights of real honor, strive to reach the kingdom of heaven. If you value rank and renown, hasten to be enrolled in the heavenly court of the angels.

Pope Gregory the Great

Ambition is the mother of hypocrisy and prefers to skulk in corners and dark places. It cannot endure the light of day. It is an unclean vice wallowing in the depths, always hidden, but ever with an eye to advancement.

Bernard of Clairvaux

ANGELS — *See also Angels, Guardian; Angels and Saints*

The whole air about us is filled with angels.

John Chrysostom

Now it was not for the angels that Christ died. Yet what was done for the redemption of man through His death was in a sense done for the angels, because the enmity that sin had put between men and the holy angels is removed, and friendship is restored between them, and by the redemption of man the gaps that the great apostasy left in the angelic host are filled up.

Augustine of Hippo

An angel is an intelligent being, ever in motion, with free will, incorporeal, ministering to God, having by grace obtained immortality in his nature, the form and limitation of whose essence is known to the Creator alone.

John of Damascus

If we saw an angel clearly, we would die of pleasure.

Bridget of Sweden

Since God often sends us inspirations by means of His angels, we should frequently return our aspirations to Him by means of the same messengers.

Frances de Sales

Make yourself familiar with the angels, and behold them frequently in spirit. Without being seen, they are present with you.

Francis de Sales

Every breath of air and ray of light and heat, every beautiful prospect, is, as it were, the skirts of their garments, the waving of the robes of those whose faces see God in heaven.

John Henry Cardinal Newman

ANGELS, GUARDIAN

Our weakness is such that, if the guardian angels had not been given to us, we could not resist the many and powerful attacks of the evil spirits. For this purpose, we had need of a higher nature.... That is why God has taken these spirits out from among His treasures, and has given through them an aid to human weakness, so that this divine assistance might help us against the powers of this world of darkness to attain the heritage of salvation.

Hilary of Poitiers

Beside each believer stands an angel as protector and shepherd, leading him to life.

Basil the Great

An angel is put in charge of every believer, provided we do not drive him out by sin. He guards the soul like an army.

Basil the Great

We pray to the angels, for they are given to us as guardians.

Ambrose of Milan

So valuable to heaven is the dignity of the human soul that every member of the human race has a guardian angel from the moment the person begins to be.

Jerome

Our deeds are daily, both day and night, reported to the Lord by the angels assigned to us.

Benedict of Nursia

They are the guardians of the divisions of the earth; they are set over nations and regions allotted to them by their Creator. They govern all our affairs and bring us help. And the reason surely is that they are set over us by the divine will and command and are ever in the vicinity of God.

John of Damascus

The world of pure spirits stretches between the Divine Nature and the world of men. Because Divine Wisdom has ordained that the higher should look after the lower, angels execute the divine plan for human salvation: They are our guardians, who free us when hindered and help to bring us home.

Thomas Aquinas

If you find it impossible to pray, hide behind your good angel and charge him to pray in your stead.

John Vianney

When tempted, invoke your angel. He is more eager to help you than you are to be helped! Ignore the devil and do not be afraid of him: He trembles and flees at the sight of your guardian angel.

John Bosco

ANGELS AND SAINTS

I tell you truly, my beloved, that our carelessness and our humiliation and our turning aside from the way are not a loss to us only, but they are a weariness for the angels and for all the saints in Jesus Christ. Our humiliation gives grief to them all, and our salvation gives joy and refreshment to them all.

Antony the Great

I bind to myself today the power in the love of the Seraphim, in the obedience of the Angels, in the ministration of the Archangels, in the hope of Resurrection unto reward, in the prayers of the Patriarchs, in the predictions of the Prophets, in the preaching of the Apostles, in the faith of the Confessors, in the purity of the holy Virgins, in the deeds of Righteous men.

Patrick of Ireland

So great was my joy in God that I took no heed of looking at the angels and the saints, because all their goodness and all their beauty was from Him and in Him; He was the whole and supreme Good, with all beauty, and so great a joy had I in His words that I paid no heed to any creature.

Angela of Foligno

I call upon the angels and saints, who fly like eagles straight toward their fiery goal; their protection will defend me against the birds of prey that threaten to devour me. The spirits of evil cannot claim me for their own; I belong only to You, Jesus, You who have Your nest up there in the sun of love.

Thérèse of Lisieux

ANGER — *See also Anger, Holy*

It is blasphemy if you pray before God while you are full of wrath.

Ephraem the Syrian

Anger is a kind of temporary madness.

Basil the Great

If an angry man raises the dead, God is still displeased with his anger.

Abba Agatho

Guard your tongue when your husband is angry.

Monica

Imagine your anger to be a kind of wild beast ... because it too has ferocious teeth and claws, and if you don't tame it, it will devastate all things.... It not only hurts the body; it even corrupts the health of the soul, devouring, rending, tearing to pieces all its strength, and making it useless for everything.

John Chrysostom

What is hatred, after all, than anger that was allowed to remain, that has become ingrained and deep-rooted? What was anger when it was fresh becomes hatred when it is aged.

Augustine of Hippo

As long as anger lives, she continues to be the fruitful mother of many unhappy children.

John Climacus

There is no sin nor wrong that gives a man such a foretaste of hell in this life as anger and impatience.

Catherine of Siena

You will accomplish more by kind words and a courteous manner than by anger or sharp rebuke, which should never be used except in necessity.

Angela Merici

This deadly cancer of anger from which so much harm grows: It makes us unlike ourselves, makes us like timber wolves or furies from hell, drives us forth headlong upon the points of swords, makes us blindly run forth after other men's destruction as we hasten toward our own ruin.

Thomas More

From what does such contrariness arise in habitually angry people, but from a secret cause of too high an opinion of themselves so that it pierces their heart when they see any man esteem them less than they esteem themselves?... An inflated estimation of ourselves is more than half the weight of our wrath.

Thomas More

If we should see two men fighting together over serious matters, we would still think them both crazy if they did not leave off fighting when they saw a ferocious lion coming toward them, ready to devour them both. Now considering that we surely see that death is coming on us all, and will undoubtedly within a short time devour us all—how soon, we don't know—isn't it worse than insanity to be angry and bear malice to one another, more often than not over trivial matters, in the same way children fight over cherry stones?

Thomas More

Dismiss all anger and look into yourself a little. Remember that he of whom you are speaking is your brother and, as he is in the way of salvation, God can make him a saint, in spite of his present weakness.

Thomas of Villanova

Why lose your temper if by doing so you offend God, annoy other people, give yourself a bad time ... and in the end have to find it again?

Josemaria Escriva

ANGER, HOLY

Reason opposes evil all the more effectively when anger resides at her side.

Pope Gregory the Great

There is a holy anger, excited by zeal, that moves us to reprove with warmth those whom our mildness failed to correct.

Jean Baptiste de la Salle

THE APOCALYPSE

Whatever has been prophesied is coming to pass, and as the end of the world approaches, it tests both men and the times.

Cyprian of Carthage

If the walls of your home were shaking with age, the roofs above you were trembling, and the house, now worn out and wearied, were threatening an immediate collapse of a structure crumbling with age, wouldn't you get out of it as quickly as possible? If you were on a voyage, and an angry, raging tempest violently aroused by the waves foretold the coming shipwreck, wouldn't you quickly seek harbor? Well, the world is changing and passing away; it witnesses to its own ruin now, not by old age, but by the end of things. So shouldn't you thank God, shouldn't you congratulate yourself, if by an early departure you're taken away and rescued from the shipwrecks and disasters that are imminent?

Cyprian of Carthage

Elijah ... will come; the Jews will believe; Antichrist will persecute; Christ will judge; the dead will rise; the good and the wicked will be separated; the world will be burned and renewed. All these things, we believe, will come to pass; but how, or in what order, human understanding cannot perfectly teach us—we will know only when we have experienced the events themselves.

Augustine of Hippo

In vain, then, do we attempt to compute definitely the years that may remain to this world, when we may hear from the mouth of the Truth Himself that it is not for us to know this.

Augustine of Hippo

APOLOGETICS

While the hot restlessness of heretics stirs questions about many articles of the Catholic faith, the necessity of defending them forces us to investigate them more accurately, to understand them more clearly, and to proclaim them more earnestly; and the question mooted by an adversary becomes the occasion of instruction.

Augustine of Hippo

My object is … to have the naked truth made known to all who are astray and to have it revealed by God's help through my ministry, commending itself so well that they may embrace and follow it.

Augustine of Hippo

Heretics are to be converted by an example of humility and other virtues far more readily than by any external display or verbal battles. So let us arm ourselves with devout prayers and set off showing signs of genuine humility and go barefooted to combat Goliath.

Dominic

Nothing is so difficult as to enter into the characters and feelings of men who have been brought up under a system of religion different from our own; and to discern how they may be most forcibly and profitably addressed, in order to win them over to the reception of divine truths, of which they are at present ignorant.

John Henry Cardinal Newman

ARIDITY, SPIRITUAL

My spirit has become dry because it forgets to feed on You.

John of the Cross

As to the aridity you are suffering from, it seems to me our Lord is treating you like someone He considers strong: He wants to test you and see if you love Him as much at times of aridity as when He sends you consolations. I think this is a very great favor for God to show you.

Teresa of Avila

Don't let aridity distress you: Perfection has nothing to do with such things—only with virtues. Your devotion will come back when you are least expecting it.

Teresa of Avila

One single act done with aridity of spirit is worth more than many done with feelings of devotion.

Francis de Sales

ART

A work of art represents the mind of the maker.

Thomas Aquinas

AUTHORITY

It is right to submit to a higher authority whenever a command of God would not be violated.

Basil the Great

When we offend those set over us, we oppose the ordinance of Him who set them above us.

Pope Gregory the Great

Men desire authority for its own sake that they may bear a rule, command and control other men, and live uncommanded and uncontrolled themselves.

Thomas More

BAD COMPANY

To know whom to avoid is a great means of saving our souls.

Thomas Aquinas

Nothing can be more dangerous than keeping wicked companions. They communicate the infection of their vices to all who associate with them.

Jean Baptiste de la Salle

If I had to advise parents, I should tell them to take great care about the people with whom their children associate.... Much harm may result from bad company, and we are inclined by nature to follow what is worse rather than what is better.

Elizabeth Ann Seton

BAPTISM

Glory be to Him who was baptized, and thus drowned our iniquity in the deep, and suffocated the one who had suffocated us!

Ephraem the Syrian

Mighty is the water in the seas, yet it is too weak for atonement; the water of baptism alone is able to atone.

Ephraem the Syrian

Today your offenses are blotted out and your names are written down. The priest blots out in the water, and Christ writes down in heaven.

Ephraem the Syrian

You who are baptized: Conquer the darkness by the light of your candles, and the silence by your hosannas!

Ephraem the Syrian

The fountain of baptism is set to protect against the flame. This is the water that avails for the quenching of hell.

Ephraem the Syrian

The diver brings up the pearl out of the sea. Be baptized and bring up from the water the purity that is hidden there, the pearl that is set like a jewel in the crown of the Godhead.

Ephraem the Syrian

The seaman stores up sweet water in his vessel; in the midst of the sea he lays up and keeps it, the sweet in the midst of the bitter. In the same way, amidst the floods of sin, keep the water of baptism.

Ephraem the Syrian

Baptism is ransom, forgiveness of debts, death of sin, regeneration of the soul, a resplendent garment, an unbreakable seal, a chariot to heaven, a royal protector, a gift of adoption.

Basil the Great

The Lord was baptized, not to be cleansed Himself, but to cleanse the waters, so that those waters, cleansed by the flesh of Christ which knew no sin, might have the power of baptism.

Ambrose of Milan

For the spirit of man is sanctified by the Spirit, when the body has been sanctified by water. For just as water, when it is poured into cauldrons and set over a blazing fire, draws power from the fire, so too by the means of the operation of the Spirit the tangible water is transformed into some divine and indescribable power, and it sanctifies those in whom it would work rebirth.

Cyril of Alexandria

Just as a man cannot live in the flesh unless he is born in the flesh, even so a man cannot have the spiritual life of grace unless he is born again spiritually. This regeneration is effected by baptism: "Unless a man is born again of water and the Holy Spirit, he cannot enter into the kingdom of God" [Jn 3:5].

Thomas Aquinas

BEAUTY

Christ has made my soul beautiful with the jewels of grace and virtue. I belong to Him whom the angels serve.

Agnes

Beauty is indeed a good gift of God; but that the good may not think it a great good, God dispenses it even to the wicked.

Augustine of Hippo

BELIEF

Understanding is the reward of faith. Therefore, don't seek to understand so that you may believe, but believe so that you may understand.

Augustine of Hippo

A person can do other things against his will, but belief is possible only in one who is willing.

Augustine of Hippo

We can't have full knowledge all at once. We must start by believing; then afterwards we may be led on to master the evidence for ourselves.

Thomas Aquinas

When someone said to him, "I don't believe in God," he smiled and replied: But God believes in you!

Padre Pio of Pietrelcina

THE BISHOP, BISHOPS

Your presbytery ... is as closely tied to the bishop as the strings to a harp. So your accord and harmonious love is a hymn to Jesus Christ. Yes, one and all, you should form yourselves into a choir, so that, in perfect harmony and taking your pitch from God, you may sing in unison and with one voice to the Father through Jesus Christ.

Ignatius of Antioch

Everyone the Master of the house sends on His business, we ought to receive as the One who sent him. It is clear, then, that we should regard the bishop as the Lord Himself.

Ignatius of Antioch

The episcopate is one, each part of which is held by each one for the whole.

Cyprian of Carthage

Be obedient to your bishop and welcome him as the parent of your soul.

Jerome

The episcopate is the title of a work, not of an honor.... He who loves to rule his flock and not be useful to his flock is no bishop.

Augustine of Hippo

Poverty is the true characteristic of a bishop.

Alphonsus Liguori

BITTERNESS

If a man cannot bear being reviled, he will not see glory. If he is not cleansed of bitterness, he will not savor sweetness.

Barsanuphius

The recollection of an injury is ... a rusty arrow and poison for the soul.

Francis of Paola

BLESSING, BLESSINGS

God is more anxious to bestow His blessings on us than we are to receive them.

Augustine of Hippo

It is not God's way that great blessings should descend without the sacrifice first of great sufferings.

John Henry Cardinal Newman

BODY, THE HUMAN

Let no one tell you that this body of ours is a stranger to God.

Cyril of Jerusalem

Don't tell me that the body is the cause of sin: After all, if the body is the cause of sin, how is it that a corpse doesn't sin? Put a sword in the right hand of someone who has just died, and no murder takes place. Let beautiful women of all kinds parade before a young man who has just died, and no lewd desire arises. Why not? Because the body of itself doesn't sin— rather, the soul sins through the body. The body is the soul's instrument, its cloak and garment.

Cyril of Jerusalem

Our body is like armor, our soul like the warrior. Take care of both, and you will be ready for what comes.

Amma Syncletice

The soul is the user, the body for use; hence the one is master, the other servant.

Ambrose of Milan

God is the Creator of the human body as well as the soul. Neither of these is evil, nor does God hate either of them: for He hates none of the things that He has made.

Augustine of Hippo

In no part of the human body visible to us is beauty sacrificed to utility, while there are some parts that serve no purpose except beauty. So I think we can readily conclude that when God created the body, He showed a greater regard for beauty than for necessity.

Augustine of Hippo

Don't ask me to give in to this body of mine. I can't afford it. Between me and my body there must be a struggle until death.

Margaret of Cortona

I have made a contract with my body: It has promised to accept harsh treatment from me on earth, and I have promised that it shall receive eternal rest in heaven.

Peter of Alcantara

One should never deny the body what is due to it, so that the body itself may not hinder what is due to the soul.

Peter of Alcantara

BOOKS

In answer to a philosopher who asked him how he could be happy without books:
My book, O philosopher, is the nature of created things, and any time I want to read the words of God, the book is before me.

Antony the Great

Never read books you aren't sure about ... even supposing that these bad books are very well written from a literary point of view. Let me ask you this: Would you drink something you knew was poisoned just because it was offered to you in a golden cup?

John Bosco

Nothing is more common in an age like this, when books abound, than to fancy that the gratification of a love of reading is real study.

John Henry Cardinal Newman

It is our duty to live among books; especially to live by one Book, and a very old one.

John Henry Cardinal Newman

I have my room, some books, and a nearby chapel. That is complete happiness.

Miguel of Ecuador

CATECHESIS

The task of the catechist is to take up one or other of the truths of faith or of Christian morality, and then explain it in all its parts; and since amendment of life is the chief aim of his instruction, the catechist must needs make a comparison between what God commands us to do and what is our actual conduct. After this, he will use examples appropriately taken from the Holy Scriptures, Church history, and the lives of the saints—thus moving his hearers and clearly pointing out to them how they are to regulate their own conduct.

Pope Pius X

CATHOLIC, CATHOLICS, CATHOLICISM

Christian is my name, and Catholic my surname. The one designates me, while the other manifests me for what I am. Thus am I attested and set apart.... When we are called Catholics, it is by this name that our people are kept apart from any heretical name.

Pacianus of Barcelona

He is a true and genuine Catholic who loves the truth of God, the Church, and the Body of Christ; who puts nothing else before divine religion and the Catholic faith, neither the authority nor the love nor the genius nor the eloquence nor the philosophy of any man whatsoever; but, despising all that and being fixed, stable, and persevering in his faith, is determined in himself to hold and believe that only which he knows the Catholic Church has held universally and from ancient times.

Vincent of Lerins

He cannot be accounted a Catholic who does not agree with the Roman Church.

Pope Gregory VII

No one can be a Catholic without a simple faith that what the Church declares in God's name is God's word, and therefore true. A man must simply believe that the Church is the oracle of God; he must be as certain of her mission as he is of the mission of the Apostles.

John Henry Cardinal Newman

Catholicism is a deep matter, you cannot take it up in a tea-cup.

John Henry Cardinal Newman

In the long run it will be found that either the Catholic religion is verily and indeed the coming in of the unseen world into this, or that there is nothing positive, nothing dogmatic, nothing real in any of our notions as to whence we come and whither we are going.

John Henry Cardinal Newman

CHANGE

Let nothing disturb you, nothing frighten you; all things are passing; God never changes.

Teresa of Avila

Well and good if all things change, Lord God, provided we are rooted in You.

John of the Cross

In a higher world it is otherwise; but here below, to live is to change, and to be perfect is to have changed often.

John Henry Cardinal Newman

CHARITY — *See also Love; Loving God*

He who has charity is far from all sin.

Polycarp of Smyrna

Charity is the bond of brotherhood, the foundation of peace, the mainstay and security of unity, which is greater than both hope and faith, which excels both good works and martyrdom, which will abide with us always, eternal with God in the kingdom of heaven.

Cyprian of Carthage

I define charity as a motion of the soul whose purpose is to enjoy God for His own sake and oneself and one's neighbor for the sake of God.

Augustine of Hippo

Charity is the form, mover, mother, and root of all the virtues.

Thomas Aquinas

It can only be disgraceful for some Christians to snore while other Christians are in peril.

Thomas More

Charity is that with which no one is lost, and without which no one is saved.

Robert Cardinal Bellarmine

The school of Christ is the school of charity. On the last day, when the general examination takes place, there will be no question at all on the text of Aristotle, the aphorisms of Hippocrates, or the paragraphs of Justinian. Charity will be the whole syllabus.

Robert Cardinal Bellarmine

True virtue has no limits, but goes on and on, and especially holy charity, which is the virtue of virtues, and which, having an infinite object, would become infinite if it could meet with a heart capable of infinity.

Francis de Sales

CHASTITY

Don't say that you have a chaste mind if you have unchaste eyes, because an unchaste eye is the messenger of an unchaste heart.

Augustine of Hippo

A prayer of his youth while he was still resisting God:
Give me chastity and continence—but not yet.

Augustine of Hippo

CHEERFULNESS

Cheerfulness prepares a glorious mind for all the noblest acts of religion—love, adoration, praise, and every union with our God, as also for duties, charity, happy zeal, useful concern for our neighbor, and all those acts of piety which should improve cheerfulness, and dispose the poor soul to joyful serenity—resting all upon infinite goodness!

Elizabeth Ann Seton

CHILDREN — *See also the Family; Marriage*

Better to instruct a child than to collect riches.

Herve of Brittany

Both the raven and the ape think their own young the fairest.

Thomas More

Children should never be taken to church in dress that would not be thought good enough for appearing before company.

Jean Baptiste de la Salle

I imagine that the angels themselves, if they came down as schoolmasters, would find it hard to control their anger. Only with the help of the Blessed Virgin do I keep from murdering some of them.

Benildus

You can do nothing with children unless you win their confidence and love by bringing them into touch with yourself, by breaking through all the hindrances that keep them at a distance. We must accommodate ourselves to their tastes, we must make ourselves like them.

John Bosco

A child is a pledge of immortality, for he bears upon him in figure those high and eternal excellences in which the joy of heaven consists, and which would not thus be shadowed forth by the all-gracious Creator, were they not one day to be realized.

John Henry Cardinal Newman

My Lord, if it is necessary to give them a whipping or two to convert them, please do it, as long as their souls are saved in the end.

Padre Pio of Pietrelcina

CHRIST — *See also Jesus*

Jesus Christ, our Salvation, the High Priest of our offerings, the Protector and Helper of our weakness. Through Him we fix our gaze on the heights of heaven. In Him we see mirrored God's pure and transcendent Face.

Pope Clement I

Blessed be the Fruit, who lowered Himself to our famished state!

Ephraem the Syrian

When we speak about wisdom, we are speaking of Christ. When we speak about virtue, we are speaking of Christ. When we speak about justice, we are speaking of Christ. When we speak about peace, we are speaking of Christ. When we speak about truth and life and redemption, we are speaking of Christ.

Ambrose of Milan

Christ with me, Christ before me, Christ behind me, Christ within me, Christ below me, Christ above me, Christ at my right, Christ at my left, Christ in lying down, Christ in sitting, Christ in rising up, Christ in the heart of every man who thinks of me, Christ in the mouth of every man who speaks to me, Christ in every eye that sees me, Christ in every ear that hears me.

Patrick of Ireland

The Creator and Lord of all so loved the world, that He sent His Son for its salvation, the Prince and Savior of the faithful, who washed and dried our wounds, and from Him also came that most sweet medicine, from which all the good things of salvation flow.

Hildegard of Bingen

If, then, you are looking for the way by which you should go, take Christ, because He Himself is the way.

Thomas Aquinas

He belongs to you, but more than that, He longs to be in you, living and ruling in you, as the head lives and rules in the body. He wants His breath to be in your breath, His heart in your heart, and His soul in your soul.

John Eudes

CHRIST, THE BLOOD OF

Where they see the Blood of the Lord, demons flee while angels gather.

John Chrysostom

This Blood, poured out in abundance, has washed the whole world clean.

John Chrysostom

Those who share in this Blood have taken their stand with angels, and archangels, and the powers from on high, clad in the royal uniform of Christ with spiritual weapons in their hands. Yet greater still than that: They are wearing the King Himself!

John Chrysostom

This is the price of the world; by it, Christ purchased the Church; by it, He adorned her entirely. Just as a man in buying slaves pays for them in gold and then, if he desires to beautify them, ornaments them with gold as well, so also Christ has both purchased us with His Blood and adorned us with His Blood.

John Chrysostom

Blood that but one drop of has the power to win
All the world forgiveness of its world of sin.

Thomas Aquinas

CHRIST, THE BODY OF

Christ has no body on earth but yours, no hands but yours, no feet but yours. Yours are the eyes through which Christ's compassion for the world is to look out; yours are the feet with which He is to go about doing good; and yours are the hands with which He is to bless us now.

Teresa of Avila

CHRIST, THE PASSION OF

His face endured spitting, so that you might not shrink from scorn....
Endure scorn from your brother, so that you may be the companion of Christ.

Ephraem the Syrian

Death's pallid hue comes o'er You; the glow of life decays;
Yet angel hosts adore You, and tremble as they gaze.

Bernard of Clairvaux

What language shall I borrow to thank Thee, dearest Friend,
For this, Thy dying sorrow, Thy pity without end?
O make me Thine forever, and should I fainting be,
Lord, let me never, never outlive my love for Thee!

Bernard of Clairvaux

You should carry the passion of God in your hearts, for it is man's consolation in his last hour.

Nicholas of Flue

The Church has always taught that all our penance without Christ's passion is not worth a pea.

Thomas More

Here learn the science of the saints: All is to be found in the passion of Jesus. Make every effort to remain hidden in the wounds of Jesus, and you will be enriched with every good and every true light, enabling you to fly to that Perfection which is consonant with your way of life.

Paul of the Cross

The passion of Jesus is a sea of sorrows, but it is also an ocean of love. Ask the Lord to teach you to fish in this ocean. Dive into its depths. No matter how deep you go, you will never reach the bottom.

Paul of the Cross

Make a little bouquet of the sufferings of Jesus and carry them in the bosom of the soul.

Paul of the Cross

Mount Calvary is the academy of love.

Francis de Sales

CHRIST, THE POWER OF

I bind to myself today
The might of the Incarnation of Christ with that of His Baptism,
The might of His Crucifixion with that of His Burial,
The might of His Resurrection with that of His Ascension,
The might of His Coming on the Judgment Day.

Patrick of Ireland

THE CHRIST CHILD

Blessed be the Babe who made manhood young again today!

Ephraem the Syrian

How astonished I am that there is laid before me a Child who is older than all things!

Ephraem the Syrian

The Child, the Lord Jesus Christ ... Word in our flesh, Wisdom in infancy, Power in weakness, and in true Man, the Lord of Majesty.

Pope Leo the Great

May He make us children of God, He who for our sakes wished to become a Child of man.

Augustine of Hippo

CHRISTIANS, CHRISTIANITY

Christianity is an imitation of God's nature.

Gregory of Nyssa

Imagine that a professional painter is commissioned to paint a portrait of the king for those who live far away. What if he draws an ugly caricature on the wood and calls this ungracious picture an image of the king? Wouldn't it be likely that the authorities would be annoyed because the handsome original had been insulted through this bad portrait as it was viewed among those who had never seen the king? In a similar way, then, if ... Christianity is an imitation of God, the person who has never been given an explanation of this mystery will assume that God is like us Christians.

Gregory of Nyssa

Since He is the Sun of Justice, He fittingly calls His disciples the light of the world. For through them, as through shining rays, He has poured out the light of the knowledge of Himself upon the entire world. For by manifesting the light of truth, they have dispelled the darkness of error from the hearts of men.

Chromatius of Aquileia

In the lives of Christians we look not to the beginnings but to the endings.

Jerome

To be a Christian is the great thing, not merely to seem one. And some-how or other those please the world most who please Christ least.

Jerome

A true Christian may almost be defined as one who has a ruling sense of God's presence within him.

John Henry Cardinal Newman

CHRISTMAS

All days from the treasure of this bright day gain blessings. All the feasts from the stores of this feast have their fairness and their ornaments.... Great is this day above all days, for in it came forth mercy to sinners. A medicine chest is this Your great day, because on it shone forth the Medicine of life to the wounded. A treasure of helpful graces is this day, because on it, Light gleamed forth on our blindness. Yes, it also brought a Sheaf to us, and it came, so that from it, plenty might flow upon our hunger.

Ephraem the Syrian

In this night of reconciliation, let none be angry or gloomy. In this night that stills everything, let nothing threaten or disturb. This night belongs to the sweet One; let nothing bitter or harsh be in it. In this night that belongs to the meek One, let there be nothing high or haughty. In this day of pardoning, let us not exact punishments for trespasses. In this day of gladness, let us not spread sadness.... In this day when God came to sinners, let not the righteous man be in his own mind uplifted over the sinner.

Ephraem the Syrian

In this day in which the Rich became poor for our sakes, let the rich man make the poor man share with him at his table. On this day came forth to us the Gift, even though we had not asked for it! Let us therefore bestow alms on those who cry and beg from us.

Ephraem the Syrian

Today Godhead pressed itself like a seal upon manhood, so that with the Godhead's stamp, manhood might be adorned.

Ephraem the Syrian

Christ is born, so that by His birth He might restore your nature.

Peter Chrysologus

Celebrate the feast of Christmas every day, even every moment in the interior temple of your spirit, remaining like a baby in the bosom of the heavenly Father, where you will be reborn each moment in the Divine Word, Jesus Christ.

Paul of the Cross

CHURCH, THE CATHOLIC — *See also Church, the Permanence of the Catholic; Church, the Unity of the Catholic*

Where the bishop is, there let the people gather, just as where Jesus Christ is, there is the Catholic Church.

Ignatius of Antioch

Where the Church is, there is the Spirit of God; and where the Spirit of God is, there is the Church and all grace—and the Spirit is truth.

Irenaeus of Lyons

We should not seek from others for the truth that can easily be received from the Church. There the apostles, like a rich man making a deposit, fully bestowed upon her all that belongs to the truth, so that whoever wishes may receive from her the water of life.

Irenaeus of Lyons

She is the entrance to life; all the others are thieves and robbers.

Irenaeus of Lyons

The very tradition, teaching, and faith of the Catholic Church from the beginning, which the Lord gave, was preached by the apostles and was preserved by the Fathers. On this was the Church founded, and if anyone departs from this, he neither is, nor any longer ought to be called, a Christian.

Athanasius of Alexandria

You cannot have God for your Father if you don't have the Church for your mother.

Cyprian of Carthage

From her womb we are born, by her milk we are nourished, by her Spirit we are made alive.

Cyprian of Carthage

It is the peculiar property of the Church that when she is buffeted, she is triumphant; when she is assaulted with argument she proves herself in the right; when she is deserted by her supporters, she holds the field.

Hilary of Poitiers

He who sees the Church looks directly at Christ—Christ building and increasing by the addition of the elect.

Gregory of Nyssa

The establishment of the Church is a re-creation of the world.

Gregory of Nyssa

Christ and the Church are two in one flesh.

Augustine of Hippo

Your mother is the Church, and her breasts are the two Testaments of the divine Scriptures. Suckle them to drink the milk of all the sacraments.

Augustine of Hippo

The Catholic Church is the work of divine Providence, achieved through the prophecies of the prophets, through the Incarnation and the teaching of Christ, through the journeys of the apostles, through the suffering, the crosses, the blood and death of the martyrs, through the admirable lives of the saints.... When we see, then, so much help on God's part, so much progress and so much fruit, shall we hesitate to bury ourselves in the bosom of that Church? For beginning with the apostolic chair, down through successions of bishops, even to the open confession of all mankind, it has possessed the crown of teaching authority.

Augustine of Hippo

Anyone who is outside this Church, which received the keys of the kingdom of heaven, is walking a path not to heaven but to hell.... Let them hasten, then, while there is yet time, to their legitimate Mother, who legitimately sustains and nourishes the sons born of her womb.

Fulgence of Ruspe

The teaching of the Church ... is both the starting line and the finish line for the race; it is the bridle of a tightly reined horse.

John of Damascus

The Church is like a great ship being pounded by the waves of life's different stresses. Our duty is not to abandon ship, but to keep her on her course.

Boniface of Mainz

There is but one Church in which men find salvation, just as outside the ark of Noah it was not possible for anyone to be saved.

Thomas Aquinas

Just as in one man there is one soul and one body, yet many members; even so the Catholic Church is one body, having many members. The soul that quickens this body is the Holy Spirit; and therefore in the Creed after confessing our belief in the Holy Spirit, we are bid to believe in the Holy Catholic Church.

Thomas Aquinas

To Pope Gregory XI:
Since the Church began aiming more at temporal things than at spiritual, things have gone from bad to worse.

Catherine of Siena

Comfort in tribulation can be secured only on the sure ground of faith holding as true the words of Scripture and the teaching of the Catholic Church.

Thomas More

Either Christ has a Church in the world continually and until the end of the world, or else He has a Church sometimes, and sometimes not at all.

Could we think that He had a Church while He was here Himself, and perhaps awhile after, but—mysteriously—none since?... No ... that can in no way be, since He must necessarily still preserve His Church somewhere; otherwise, how could He be with His followers continually until the end of the world?

Thomas More

If we wish to proceed securely in all things, we must hold fast to the following principle: What seems to me white, I will believe black if the hierarchical Church so defines. For I must be convinced that in Christ our Lord, the Bridegroom, and in His spouse the Church, only one Spirit holds sway, who governs and rules for the salvation of souls. For it is by the same Spirit and Lord who gave the Ten Commandments that our Holy Mother Church is ruled and governed.

Ignatius Loyola

Holy Church—that Mother who is also a Queen because she is a King's bride.

Thérèse of Lisieux

Divine assistance for the Church is not restricted to the first centuries of the Church, but is continued and will be continued to the end of time. This reflection has calmed my spirit on more than one occasion. May it serve to calm yours when you witness error worming its way about.

Dominic Barberi

I will go peaceably and firmly to the Catholic Church: for if Faith is so important to our salvation, I will seek it where true Faith first began, seek it among those who received it from God Himself.

Elizabeth Ann Seton

There are but two ways, the way to Rome and the way to atheism.

John Henry Cardinal Newman

CHURCH, THE PERMANENCE OF THE
CATHOLIC — *See also Church, the Catholic*

This is holy Church, the one Church, the true Church, the Catholic Church, fighting against all heresies; she can fight, but she cannot be conquered. All heresies are expelled from her as if they were dead branches pruned from the vine; she herself, however, remains fixed in her root, in her vine, in her charity. The gates of hell shall not prevail against her.

Augustine of Hippo

The Church has ever proved indestructible. Her persecutors have failed to destroy her; in fact, it was during times of persecution that the Church grew more and more; while the persecutors themselves, and those whom the Church would destroy, are the very ones who came to nothing.... Again, errors have assailed her; but in fact, the greater the number of errors that have arisen, the more has the truth been made manifest.... Nor has the Church failed before the assaults of demons: for she is like a tower of refuge to all who fight against the Devil.

Thomas Aquinas

When [Christianity] dies, at least the world will die with it. The world's duration is measured by it. If the Church dies, the world's time is run. The world shall never exult over the [demise of the] Church. If the Church falls sick, the world shall utter a wail for its own sake; for, like Samson, the Church will bury all with it.

John Henry Cardinal Newman

CHURCH, THE UNITY OF THE CATHOLIC
— See also Church, the Catholic

God is One and Christ is One, and one is His Church, and the faith is one, and His people welded together by the glue of concord into a solid unity of body. Unity cannot be rent asunder; nor can the one body of the Church, through the division of its structure, be divided into separate pieces.

Cyprian of Carthage

His Church is one, His see is one, founded by the voice of the Lord on Peter. No other altar can be set up, no other priesthood instituted apart from that one altar and that one priesthood. Whoever gathers elsewhere, scatters.

Cyprian of Carthage

In the Scriptures our people are shown to be made one; so that just as many grains collected into one and ground and mingled together make one loaf, so in Christ, who is the heavenly Bread, we know there is one body, in which our whole company is joined and united.

Hilary of Poitiers

Hold firmly that our faith is identical with that of the ancients. Deny this, and you dissolve the unity of the Church.

Thomas Aquinas

COMMUNION, DAILY — *See also Eucharist*

If it is "daily bread," why do you take it once a year?... Take daily what is to profit you daily. Live in such a way that you may deserve to receive it daily. He who does not deserve to receive it daily, does not deserve to receive it once a year.

Ambrose of Milan

We can afford to lose castles, but we cannot let a day go by without attending holy Mass.

Charles of Blois

If someone knows from experience that daily Communion increases fervor without lessening reverence, then let him go every day. But if someone finds that reverence is lessened and devotion not much increased, then let him sometimes abstain, so as to draw near afterwards with better dispositions.

Thomas Aquinas

There is neither past nor present nor future for Jesus Christ. This good Father knew us all at the Last Supper. He consecrated, as it were in thought and in desire, all our Hosts; He loved us personally ... centuries before we were born. Yes, we were present at the Last Supper, and Jesus stored up for us not one Host but a hundred, a thousand, one for every day of our life.... Our Hosts are ready; let us not lose a single one of them.

Peter Julian Eymard

Keep up your daily Communion and think: What would I be if I had not gone?

Josemaria Escriva

THE COMMUNION OF SAINTS— *See also Saints*

If the apostles and martyrs while still in the body can pray for others, at a time when they should still be solicitous about themselves, how much more will they do so after their crowns, victories, and triumphs?

Jerome

What do they not see, who see Him who sees all things?

Pope Gregory the Great

Just as in a physical body the operation of one member contributes to the good of the whole body, so it is in a spiritual body such as the Church. And since all the faithful are one body, the good of one member is communicated to another; *every one members,* as the Apostle says, *of one another* [Eph 4:25]. For that reason, among the points of faith handed down by the Apostles, is that there is a community of goods in the Church, and this is expressed in the words *communion of saints.*

Thomas Aquinas

The greater the charity of the saints in their heavenly home, the more they intercede for those who are still on their journey and the more they can help them by their prayers; the more they are united with God, the more effective those prayers are. This is in accordance with divine order, which makes higher things react upon lower things, like the brightness of the sun filling the atmosphere.

Thomas Aquinas

Those in the Catholic Church, whom some rebuke for praying to saints and going on pilgrimages, do not seek any saint as their savior. Instead, they seek saints as those whom their Savior loves, and whose intercession and prayer for the seeker He will be content to hear. For His own sake, He would have those He loves honored. And when they are thus honored for His sake, then the honor that is given them for His sake overflows especially to Himself.

Thomas More

Considering that when the saints lived in this world they were at liberty to roam the earth, do you really think that in heaven God would have them tied to a post?

Thomas More

You say you see no reason why we should pray to the saints since God can hear us and help us just as well, and will do so gladly, as any saint in heaven. Well, then, what need, I ask, do you have to ask any physician to help your fever, or to ask and pay any surgeon to heal your sore leg? For God can both hear you and help you as well as the best of doctors, He loves you more than they do, and He can help you sooner. Besides—His poultices are cheaper and He will give you more for your words alone than they will for your money!

Thomas More

If Saint Paul exhorts us to pray for one another, and we gladly think it right to ask every poor man to pray for us, should we think it evil to ask the holy saints in heaven to do the same?

Thomas More

Do you think, daughters, that God comes to you all by Himself?... You may be sure that such a King is not left alone by the attendants of His court; but they attend Him, praying to Him for us, and for our welfare, because they are full of love.

Teresa of Avila

I shall be able to do much more for you in heaven than I can now while I am on earth.

Padre Pio of Pietrelcina

CONFESSION, PENANCE — *See also Repemtance*

Confession puts out the fires of hell for you.

Pacianus of Barcelona

Have you sinned? Go into church and wipe out your sin. As often as you might fall down in the marketplace, you pick yourself up again. So too, as often as you sin, repent your sin. Do not despair.

John Chrysostom

If the serpent, the Devil, bites someone secretly, he infects that person with the venom of sin. And if the one who was bitten keeps silence and does not do penance, and does not want to confess his wound to his brother and to his Master, then his brother and his Master, who have the word that will cure him, cannot very well assist him. For if the sick man is ashamed to confess his wound to the physician, medicine will not cure that to which it is not applied.

Jerome

If you want to flee from God, flee to Him instead. Flee to Him by confessing to Him; don't flee from Him by trying to hide. For you can't hide, but you can confess.

Augustine of Hippo

In failing to confess, Lord, I would only hide You from myself, not myself from You.

Augustine of Hippo

The demon which by your silence you let dwell in your heart has been killed because you confessed your sin.... Henceforth he shall never make a home in you, because you have thrown him out of doors into the open air.

Theonas

To do penance is to bewail the evil we have done, and to do no evil to bewail.

Pope Gregory the Great

Confession heals, confession justifies, confession grants pardon of sin, all hope consists in confession; in confession there is a chance for mercy.

Isidore of Seville

In the life of the body a man is sometimes sick, and unless he takes medicine, he will die. Even so in the spiritual life a man is sick on account of sin. For that reason he needs medicine so that he may be restored to health; and this grace is bestowed in the sacrament of Penance.

Thomas Aquinas

Three conditions are necessary for Penance: contrition, which is sorrow for sin, together with a purpose of amendment; confession of sins without any omission; and satisfaction by means of good works.

Thomas Aquinas

The minister to whom confession is made is the delegate of Christ, who is the Judge of the living and the dead.

Thomas Aquinas

Go to your confessor; open your heart to him; display to him all the recesses of your soul; take the advice that he will give you with the utmost humility and simplicity. For God, who has an infinite love for obedience, frequently renders profitable the counsels we take from others, but especially from those who are the guides of our souls.

Francis de Sales

My children, when we have a little stain on our souls, we must do like someone who has a beautiful crystal globe of which she takes great care. If the globe gets a little dusty, when she sees it, she will pass a sponge over it, and there is the globe bright and shining again.

John Vianney

A person who is suffering from a slight illness ... has no need to go and see a doctor; she can get well alone.... But if it is a serious illness, if it is a dangerous wound, then the doctor must be called in, and after the doctor come the medicines. When we have fallen into some grave sin, we must go to the doctor, who is the priest, and take the medicine, which is confession.

John Vianney

Our Lord Himself I saw in ... this venerable Sacrament.... I felt as if my chains fell, as those of St. Peter at the touch of the divine messenger. My God, what new scenes for my soul!

Elizabeth Ann Seton

CONFIRMATION

Just as those who are born in the body need to be fortified so that the body may become operative, even so those who are reborn in the spirit need to be fortified by the Holy Spirit. For this reason, so that they might become strong, the apostles received the Holy Spirit after Christ's ascension.... This power is conferred in the sacrament of Confirmation.

Thomas Aquinas

Those who have charge of children ought to be most careful to see that they be confirmed, because great grace is bestowed in Confirmation. Besides, one who is confirmed receives, when he dies, greater glory than one who has not been confirmed, because he has received more grace.

Thomas Aquinas

CONSCIENCE

Look into the hiding places of your own conscience.

Cyprian of Carthage

Conscience and reputation are two things. Conscience is due to yourself; reputation is due to your neighbor.

Augustine of Hippo

God's law enters our mind and draws it to itself by stirring up conscience, which itself is called the law of our mind.

John of Damascus

The testimony of a man's conscience is his only perfect and complete excuse.

Bernard of Clairvaux

A good conscience is a mine of wealth. And in truth what greater riches can there be, what thing more sweet, than a good conscience?

Bernard of Clairvaux

Jesus Christ loves to rest in pure and tranquil consciences.

Henry Suso

God desires from you the least degree of purity of conscience more than all the works you can perform.

John of the Cross

My conscience is my crown; contented thoughts my rest;
My heart is happy in itself; my bliss is in my breast.

Robert Southwell

Conscience has rights because it has duties.

John Henry Cardinal Newman

Conscience is nearer to me than any other means of knowledge.

John Henry Cardinal Newman

CONSOLATIONS, SPIRITUAL

Perfection does not consist in consolation, but rather in the submission of
the will to God alone; submission above all in things that are hard and bitter.

Henry Suso

I call it consolation when an interior movement is stirred up in the soul, by
which it is set on fire with love of its Creator and Lord, and as a consequence can love no creature on the face of the earth for its own sake, but
only in the Creator of them all. It is likewise consolation when we shed
tears that move us to love God, whether it is because of sorrow for sins, or
because of the sufferings of Christ our Lord, or for any other reason that is
immediately directed to the praise and service of God. Finally, I call consolation every increase of faith, hope, and charity, and all interior joy that
invites and attracts us to what is heavenly and to the salvation of our soul
by filling it with peace and quiet in its Creator and Lord.

Ignatius Loyola

There are certain souls who are always looking for consolation in prayer;
this is a delusion of the Devil, who simply wishes to bring about their
destruction.

Alphonsus Liguori

When you have no consolations, you serve God for Himself alone; but
when you have them you're liable to serve Him out of love for yourself.

John Vianney

CONTEMPLATION

The contemplation of God is promised to us as the goal of all our acts and the eternal consummation of all our joys.

Augustine of Hippo

The greatness of contemplation can be given to none but those who love.

Pope Gregory the Great

The grace of contemplation is granted only in response to a longing and insistent desire.

Bernard of Clairvaux

When you have stabilized your heart in right faith, and steadfast hope, and perfect love, then you will heave up your heart in high contemplation of your Creator.

Edmund of Abingdon

Better to illuminate than merely to shine, to deliver to others contemplated truths than merely to contemplate.

Thomas Aquinas

Contemplation is nothing else than a secret, peaceful, and loving infusion of God, which if admitted, will set the soul on fire with the Spirit of love.

John of the Cross

CONTEMPLATION AND ACTION

Whoever wishes to hold the fortress of contemplation must first of all train in the camp of action.

Pope Gregory the Great

We ascend to the heights of contemplation by the steps of action.

Pope Gregory the Great

In the active life all the vices are first of all to be removed by the practice of good works, so that in the contemplative life a man may, with now purified mental gaze, pass on to the contemplation of the divine Light.

Isidore of Seville

CONVERSION, CONVERTS

There are in truth three states of the converted: the beginning, the middle, and the perfection. In the beginning they experience the charms of sweetness; in the middle the contests of temptation; and in the end the fullness of perfection.

Pope Gregory the Great

Heaven is filled with converted sinners of all kinds, and there is room for more.

Joseph Cafasso

First let a little love find entrance into their hearts, and the rest will follow.

Philip Neri

You can win more converts with a spoonful of honey than with a barrelful of vinegar.

Francis de Sales

A convert is undeniably in favor with no party; he is looked at with distrust, contempt, and aversion by all. His former friends think him a good riddance, and his new friends are cold and strange; and as to the impartial public, their very first impression is to impute the change to some eccentricity of character, or fickleness of mind, or tender attachment, or private interest. Their utmost praise is the reluctant confession that "doubtless he is very sincere."

John Henry Cardinal Newman

CORRECTION AND EXHORTATION, MUTUAL

We must accept correction, beloved, and no one should resent it. The exhortations by which we admonish one another are both good and highly profitable, for they bind us to the will of God.

Pope Clement I

Reprimand and rebuke should be accepted as healing remedies for vice and as conducive to good health. From this it is clear that those who pretend to be tolerant because they wish to flatter—those who thus fail to correct sinners—actually cause them to suffer supreme loss and plot the destruction of that life which is their true life.

Basil the Great

Eating and drinking don't make friendships—such friendship even robbers and murderers have. But if we are friends, if we truly care for one another, let's help one another spiritually.... Let's hinder those things that lead our friends away to hell.

John Chrysostom

Don't imagine that you love your children when you never discipline them, or that you love your neighbors when you never admonish them. This isn't love, but mere weakness. Let your love be eager to correct, to reform.

Augustine of Hippo

Sometimes hatred is charming, while love must show itself severe.

Augustine of Hippo

The better friends you are, the straighter you can talk, but while you are only on nodding terms, be slow to scold.

Francis Xavier

Never rebuke while you're still indignant about a fault committed—wait until the next day, or even longer. Then calmly, and with a purer intention, make your reprimand. You'll gain more by a friendly word than by a three-hour quarrel.

Josemaria Escriva

COSMETICS

The apostate angels taught us to paint the eyes with blackness drawn round them in a circle, and to stain the cheeks with a deceitful red, and to change the hair with false colors, and to mask all truth about the real appearance of face and head.... God says, "Let us make man in our image and likeness"; does anyone dare to alter and change what God has made? They are laying hands on God when they try to reform what He has formed.

Cyprian of Carthage

Suppose an artist paints in beautiful lines and colors the likeness of someone's face and form. Then, once the portrait is completed, someone else comes along, picks it up and, thinking that he could do a better job, makes changes in the picture. Wouldn't that be a serious wrong to the first artist, and a good reason for him to be indignant? And do you think it likely you could get away with acting the same way, with a rash and wicked presumption that offends God—the Artist who created you?

Cyprian of Carthage

By dyeing your hair the color of flame, you make it a terrible foreshadowing of the fiery judgment that awaits you!

Cyprian of Carthage

COURAGE, FORTITUDE

Fortitude is the disposition of soul that enables us to despise all inconveniences and the loss of things not in our power.

Augustine of Hippo

The principal act of courage is to endure and withstand dangers doggedly rather than to attack them.

Thomas Aquinas

Though the path is plain and smooth for men of good will, he who walks it will not travel far, and will do so only with difficulty, if he does not have good feet: that is, courage and a persevering spirit.

John of the Cross

Courage! In the spiritual life, whoever doesn't go forward goes backward. It's the same as with a boat that must always go forward. If it stands still, the wind will blow it back.

Padre Pio of Pietrelcina

COVETOUSNESS, GREED

Greed will demand of you labor, danger, hardships, and troubles, and you will readily agree to its demands. For what purpose? So you can have what will fill up your purse but empty out your peace of mind!

Augustine of Hippo

It is wrong for anyone to be anxious to receive more from his neighbor than he himself is willing to give to God.

Francis of Assisi

Covetousness is like fire: the more wood that is fed to it, the more fervent and greedy it is.

Thomas More

The covetous claim to be Christian, yet they have no trust in Christ. For they are always afraid of want in the time to come, no matter how much they have.

Thomas More

This covetous gathering and miserly keeping of wealth, with all the delight that we take in beholding it, is only a very gay and golden dream, in which we imagine we have great riches; and in the sleep of this life we are glad and proud of it. But when death has once awakened us, our dream shall vanish, and of all the treasure that we only dreamed about, we shall not find one penny left in our hand.

Thomas More

I have heard thousands of confessions, but never one of covetousness.

Francis Xavier

THE CREATION, CREATURES

Creation is a great book. Look above you; look below you! Note it; read it! God ... didn't write that book with ink. Instead, He set before your eyes the things that He had made. Can you ask for a louder voice than that? Why, heaven and earth cry out to you, "God made me!"

Augustine of Hippo

Even the tiniest insect cannot be considered attentively without astonishment and without praising the Creator.

Augustine of Hippo

All creatures have the same Source as we have. Like us, they derive the life of thought, love, and will from the Creator. Not to hurt our humble brethren is our first duty to them; but to stop there is a complete misapprehension of the intentions of Providence. We have a higher mission. God wishes that we should succor them whenever they require it.

Francis of Assisi

If there is anyone who is not enlightened by this sublime magnificence of created things, he is blind.... If there is anyone who, seeing all these works of God, does not praise Him, he is dumb; if there is anyone who, from so many signs, cannot perceive God, that man is foolish.

Bonaventure

In everything, whether it is a thing sensed or a thing known, God Himself is hidden within.

Bonaventure

God passes through the thicket of the world, and wherever His glance falls He turns all things to beauty.

John of the Cross

Listen to the sermon preached to you by the flowers, the trees, the shrubs, the sky, and the whole world. Notice how they preach to you a sermon full of love, of praise of God, and how they invite you to glorify the sublimity of that sovereign Artist who has given them being.

Paul of the Cross

The other day ... the little birds were singing in the woods. I began to weep. Poor little creatures, I thought within myself, the good God has made you to sing, and you sing. Yet man, who was created that he might love God, loves Him not!

John Vianney

THE CREED

Know the Creed and the Our Father yourselves and teach them to your children. I do not know how a man can call himself a Christian ... when he neglects to learn the few short lines of the Creed or the Our Father.

Caesarius of Arles

THE CROSS, CROSSES

Glory be to You, who laid your Cross as a bridge over death, that souls might pass over it from the dwelling of the dead to the dwelling of life!

Ephraem the Syrian

Faithful Cross, above all other, one and only noble tree ... Sweet the wood, and sweet the iron, and thy load, most sweet is He.

Venantius Fortunatus

Through the Cross the nations were caught as in a net, and the seeds of faith were sown everywhere. With the Cross, as though with a plow, the disciples of Christ cultivated the unfruitful nature of mankind, revealed the

Church's ever-green pastures, and gathered in an abundant harvest of believers in Christ. By the Cross the martyrs were strengthened, and as they fell they smote down those who struck them. Through the Cross Christ became known, and the Church of the faithful, with the Scriptures ever open before her, introduces us to this same Christ, the Son of God, who is truly God and truly Lord.

Andrew of Crete

Once as the tree of torture known—now the bright gate to Jesus' throne.

Peter Damian

If you were the handsomest and the richest man in the world, and could work wonders and drive out devils, all that would be something extrinsic to you; it would not belong to you and you could not boast of it. But there is one thing of which we can boast; we can boast of our humiliations and in taking up daily the holy cross of our Lord Jesus Christ.

Francis of Assisi

The law that is perfect because it takes away all imperfections is charity, and you find it written with a strange beauty when you gaze at Jesus your Savior stretched out like a sheet of parchment on the Cross, inscribed with wounds, illustrated in His own loving blood. Where else ... is there a comparable book of love to read from?

Jordan of Saxony

The Cross possesses such power and strength that, whether they will or not, it attracts, draws, and ravishes those who carry it.

Henry Suso

However much we do to avoid them, we shall never lack crosses in this life if we are in the ranks of the Crucified.

Teresa of Avila

Be proud that you are helping God to bear the Cross, and don't grasp at comforts. It is only mercenaries who expect to be paid by the day. Serve Him without pay.

Teresa of Avila

Whoever doesn't seek the cross of Christ doesn't seek the glory of Christ.

John of the Cross

The Cross is the way to paradise, but only when it is borne willingly.

Paul of the Cross

In uniting yourself to God's will, you take on new life and gather great courage, willingly embracing the cross and kissing His hand even when it chastises you, a hand that reaches out to you in love and has no other intention but your greater spiritual well-being.

Paul of the Cross

The Cross is the ladder to heaven.

John Vianney

On the road to the Cross, it's only the first few yards that hurt.

John Vianney

Put a good bunch of grapes under the winepress, and a delicious juice will come out. Under the winepress of the Cross, our soul produces a juice that feeds and strengthens us. When we haven't got any crosses, we are dry: If we carry them with resignation, what happiness, what sweetness we feel!

John Vianney

Contrarieties bring us to the foot of the Cross, and the Cross to the gate of heaven.

John Vianney

Crosses release us from this world, and by doing so, bind us to God.

Charles de Foucauld

THE DEAD, PRAYERS FOR

In charity, follow the deceased with sorrow and with offerings, and pray that he may have rest in the hidden place where he is going.

Ephraem the Syrian

We have loved them during life; let us not abandon them until we have conducted them by our prayers into the house of the Lord.

Ambrose of Milan

The whole Church observes the custom handed down by our fathers: that those who have died within the fellowship of Christ's body and blood should be prayed for when they are commemorated in their own place at the Holy Sacrifice, and that we should be reminded that this sacrifice is offered for them as well. When these acts of mercy are solemnly performed for their sake, who can doubt that we are truly giving them our support? The prayers we offer to God for them are not futile. We must not waver in our belief that they are profitable to the dead, to those of the dead at least who have lived in such a way before death that these things can be useful to them afterward.

Augustine of Hippo

On the death of Pope St. Pius X:
I believe that his holy soul has no need of our intercessory prayers, but let us pray for his eternal rest just the same, since our prayers will never go to waste.

Padre Pio of Pietrelcina

Day and night I am pursued by the same thought: One does not pray enough for the dead. Eighty thousand people die in this nation every day.

Eugenie Smet

DEATH

It is His breath that is in us, and when He wants to, He will take it away.

Pope Clement I

Fear of death is for those who aren't willing to go to Christ.

Cyprian of Carthage

How preposterous and absurd it is, that while we ask that the will of God should be done, yet when God calls and summons us from this world, we should not at once obey the command of His will! We struggle and resist, and like obstinate servants we are dragged into the presence of the Lord with sadness and grief, departing from this world only under the bondage of necessity and not with the obedience of a free will. Yet then we wish to be honored with heavenly rewards by the One to whom we come so unwillingly!

Cyprian of Carthage

Our brethren who are freed from this world by the Lord's summons are not to be mourned, since we know that they are not lost to us, but only sent on ahead of us. Departing from us, they precede us as travelers, just as navigators are accustomed to do.

Cyprian of Carthage

Death is not an ending, but a transition, and—this journey through time having been completed—a passage into eternity. Who would not hasten to better things?

Cyprian of Carthage

Let death immediately stand before your eyes, and you will never desire anything bad or worldly.

Antony the Great

Our Lord was trampled on by death, and in His turn trod out a way over death.... Death slew and was slain. Death slew the natural life; and the supernatural Life slew him.

Ephraem the Syrian

To the good man, to die is gain. The foolish fear death as the greatest of evils; the wise desire it as a rest after labors and the end of ills.

Ambrose of Milan

What is death at most? It is a journey for a season, a sleep longer than usual. If you fear death, you should also fear sleep.

John Chrysostom

On her deathbed in a foreign land, when those around her worried that she would not be buried back home with her family:
Put this body away anywhere. Don't let care about it disturb you. I ask only this of you, that you remember me at the altar of the Lord, wherever you may be.... Nothing is far from God. I need not fear that He will not know where to raise me up at the end of the world.

Monica

A perfect life is an imitation of death.

Pope Gregory the Great

If we fear death before it comes, we shall conquer it when it comes.

Pope Gregory the Great

Nothing is more certain than death, nothing more uncertain than its hour.

Anselm of Canterbury

Death, the gate of life.

Bernard of Clairvaux

Blessed be God for our sister, the death of the body.

Francis of Assisi

I find only one fault with you, Death: that you are too stingy with those who long for you, and too lavish with those who flee from you.

Catherine of Genoa

All our whole life is but a sickness without remedy, an incurable corruption. And despite all our wrapping and plastering, bandaged up to live as long as we can, in the end we undoubtedly die of that same sickness [mortality], even though another illness may never come along. So, then, if you consider this reality well, you will look upon death not as a stranger, but as a close neighbor.

Thomas More

We should never look at death as something far off; for even if he seems to be in no hurry toward us, yet we ourselves never cease to hurry toward him.

Thomas More

In whatever way we live—whether we wake or sleep, we eat or drink, we mourn or sing—all the while we are dying.

Thomas More

I saw myself dying with a desire to see God, and I knew not how to seek that life other than by dying.

Teresa of Avila

Life is to live in such a way that we are not afraid to die.

Teresa of Avila

Everything seems to me to pass so quickly ... that we must concentrate our thoughts on how to die rather than on how to live.

Teresa of Avila

Of all the things of life, a happy death is our principal concern. For if we attain that, it matters little if we lose all the rest. But if we do not attain that, nothing else is of any value.

Juniperro Serra

Don't you know that only the thoughtless and insane consider the faithful departed to be dead?

John Eudes

Happy are they who, being always on their guard against death, find themselves always ready to die.

Francis de Sales

How sweet it is to die if one has lived on the Cross!

John Vianney

Think often of death, so as to prepare for it and appraise things at their true value.

Charles de Foucauld

I am a prisoner too—with all this wide and beautiful creation before me, the restless soul longs to enjoy its liberty and rest beyond its bound. When the Father calls His child, how readily will He be obeyed!

Elizabeth Ann Seton

What he dieth, that must he be forever; as the tree falleth, so must it lie.

John Henry Cardinal Newman

You, if you are an apostle, will not have to die. You will move to a new house: That's all.

Josemaria Escriva

DEATH OF A LOVED ONE

I give thanks to Almighty God that He has not considered me unworthy to be the mother of a child admitted into the heavenly kingdom. Having left the world in the white robe of his innocence, he will rejoice in the presence of God through all eternity.

Clotilda

To a dying friend:

As your soul departs from your body, may the shining cohorts of angels hasten to greet you, the tribunal of apostles acquit you, the triumphant ranks of white-robed martyrs accompany you, the lily-bearing bands of glorious confessors surround you, the choir of virgins bring up your train with rejoicing, and in blest tranquillity may the patriarchs receive you into their loving embrace. May our Lord Jesus appear before you gentle and eager of countenance, and assign you a place amid those who stand in His presence forevermore.

Peter Damian

I can never lose one whom I have loved to the end. One to whom my soul cleaves so firmly that it can never be separated does not go away, but only goes before. Be mindful of me when you come to where I shall follow you.

Bernard of Clairvaux

Too much sorrow for the dead is the child of either self-love or rash judgment.

Robert Southwell

DECEIT

Do you hate to be deceived? Then don't deceive others.

John Chrysostom

It is not in human nature to deceive others for any long time, without in a measure deceiving ourselves also.

John Henry Cardinal Newman

DEFECTS, FAULTS

Who is free from defects? He lacks everything who thinks he lacks nothing.

Bernard of Clairvaux

Peace and union are the most necessary of all things for men who live in common, and nothing serves so well to establish and maintain these as the forbearing charity whereby we put up with one another's defects.

Robert Cardinal Bellarmine

There is no one who is without faults, and who is not in some way a burden to others, whether he is a superior or a subject, an old man or a young one, a scholar or a dunce.

Robert Cardinal Bellarmine

It's true you have defects. But is any of this any reason for losing trust in God? Could it be His Divine Majesty doesn't know that we're dirt, dust, and ashes, always inclined to evil?

Paul of the Cross

Learn to hate your faults, but to hate them calmly.

Padre Pio of Pietrelcina

DEMONS, DEVILS

However great may be the temptation, if we know how to use the weapon of prayer well we shall come off conquerors at last, for prayer is more powerful than all the devils. He who is attacked by the spirits of darkness needs only to apply himself vigorously to prayer, and he will beat them back with great success.

Bernard of Clairvaux

Even the demons were not solely responsible for crucifying Him; it was you who crucified Him with them, and you continue to crucify Him by taking pleasure in your vices and sins.

Francis of Assisi

DESIRE

Holy desire fills us only to the extent that we cut off our longings from the love of the world. You must first empty what you want to be filled. If you are to be filled with what is good, then you must pour out what is evil....
In truth, we are to be filled with Something beyond words: God Himself.

We must stretch ourselves out to Him, then, so that when He comes, He may fill us.

Augustine of Hippo

What a man desires, if he worships it, is to him a god. A vice in the heart is an idol on the altar.

Jerome

Our one desire and choice should be what is more conducive to the end for which we are created.

Ignatius Loyola

He who desires anything but God deceives himself; and he who loves anything but God errs miserably.

Philip Neri

Don't desire not to be what you are, but desire to be very well what you are.

Francis de Sales

Love heavenly desires, and desire heavenly love.

Francis de Sales

DESOLATION

O God, You seek those who hide from You, and hide from those who seek You!

Augustine of Hippo

God said to her:
I am concealing Myself from you so that you can discover by yourself what you are without Me.

Margaret of Cortona

In times of desolation you should never make a change, but stand firm in the resolutions and decisions that guided you the day before the desolation.

Ignatius Loyola

DESPAIR

We need not despair of any man, as long as he lives.

Augustine of Hippo

When tempted to despair, I have only one recourse: to throw myself at the foot of the Tabernacle like a little dog at the feet of his master.

John Vianney

If I saw the gates of hell open and I stood on the brink of the abyss, I would not despair, I would not lose hope of mercy, because I would trust in You, my God.

Gemma Galgani

However wicked I may be, however great a sinner, I *must* hope that I will go to heaven. You forbid me to despair.

Charles de Foucauld

The most beautiful Credo is the one we pronounce in our hour of darkness.

Padre Pio of Pietrelcina

DETACHMENT FROM THE WORLD
— See also World, Worldliness

Don't have Jesus Christ on your lips and the world in your hearts.

Ignatius of Antioch

Of no use will be to me the farthest reaches of the universe or the kingdoms of this world. I would rather die and come to Jesus Christ than be king over the entire earth.

Ignatius Antioch

Act as if God alone existed and nothing else.

Ephraem the Syrian

If you can discern wisely, don't exchange ... what abides for what doesn't abide, what never ceases for what ceases; nor truth for lies, nor body for shadow, nor watching for slumber, nor what is in season for what is out of season; nor the Time for the times.

Ephraem the Syrian

A great crown is laid up for you, brothers; don't barter away a great dignity for a petty pleasure.

Cyril of Jerusalem

Let us not esteem worldly prosperity or adversity as if they were real things or things of any importance, but let us live elsewhere, and raise all our attention to heaven; counting sin as the only true evil, and nothing truly good but virtue, which unites us to God.

Gregory Nazianzen

The man who has sharp vision for God alone is blind in all the other things that attract the eyes of the multitude.... Sharp-eyed and clear-sighted is the man who looks only to the good with the single eye of his soul.

Gregory of Nyssa

All the preoccupation of men with the things of this life is but the game of children on the sands.... For as soon as their labor is completed, the sand falls down and nothing is left of their buildings.

Gregory of Nyssa

As no darkness can be seen by anyone surrounded by light, so no trivialities can capture the attention of anyone who has his eyes on Christ.

Gregory of Nyssa

Whoever seeks earth before he seeks heaven will surely lose both earth and heaven.

John Chrysostom

A detached man should always be looking to see what he can do without.

Henry Suso

The whole of this present world has become mean and wearisome, and on the other hand the world to come has become so unspeakably desirable and dear that I hold all these passing things as light as thistledown.

Herman of Reichenau

Man is created to praise, reverence, and serve God our Lord, and by this means to save his soul. The other things on the face of the earth are created for man to help him in attaining the end for which he is created. Hence, man is to make use of them insofar as they help him in the attainment of his end, and he must rid himself of them insofar as they prove a hindrance to him.

Ignatius Loyola

The best thing must be to flee from all to the All.

Teresa of Avila

The soul that journeys to God, but doesn't shake off its cares and quiet its appetites, is like someone who drags a cart uphill.

John of the Cross

Give me ten truly detached men, and I will convert the world with them.

Philip Neri

The blessings He has given me ... are scorn of the world—of its pleasures, its riches, its honors; and the love of the cross, of poverty, of humility; as well as the honor of His constant presence, of familiarity and intimacy with Him, and above all the love of His love.

Marie of the Incarnation

We are pilgrims and strangers on earth. Pilgrims sleep in tents and sometimes cross deserts, but the thought of their homeland makes them forget everything else.

Charles de Foucauld

THE DEVIL, LUCIFER, SATAN

God gives the Devil power against us in two modes: either for punishment when we sin, or for glory when we are tested.

Cyprian of Carthage

Draw near to God, and Satan will flee from you.

Ephraem the Syrian

The soul possesses freedom; and though the Devil can make suggestions, he doesn't have the power to compel you against your will.

Cyril of Jerusalem

Committing sin makes us strangers to God and partners with the Devil.

Basil the Great

The Devil's snare doesn't catch you unless you're already nibbling on the Devil's bait.

Ambrose of Milan

The Devil often transforms himself into an angel to tempt men, some for their instruction and some for their ruin.

Augustine of Hippo

There's more than one way of sacrificing to the fallen angels.

Augustine of Hippo

Job was turned over to the Devil to be tempted so that, by withstanding the test, he would be a torment to the Devil.

Augustine of Hippo

The Devil has never made anyone or begotten anyone or created anyone; but whoever acts as the Devil does becomes in one sense a child of the Devil, as if begotten by him. The child resembles the father, not because they are literally kin, but because the child imitates the father.

Augustine of Hippo

We have been called to heal wounds, to unite what has fallen apart, and to bring home those who have lost their way. Many who may seem to us to be children of the Devil will still become Christ's disciples.

Francis of Assisi

When the Devil is called the god of this world, it's not because he made it, but because we serve him with our worldliness.

Thomas Aquinas

Remember that the Devil doesn't sleep, but seeks our ruin in a thousand ways.

Angela Merici

The Devil never runs upon a man to seize him with his claws until he sees him on the ground, already having fallen by his own will.

Thomas More

The strategy of our adversary can be compared to the tactics of a commander intent upon seizing and plundering a position he desires. The leader of an army will encamp, explore the fortifications and defenses of the fortress, and attack at the weakest point. In the same way, the adversary of our human nature examines from every side all our virtues, theological, cardinal, and moral. Wherever he discovers the defenses of eternal salvation to be the weakest and most lacking, there he attacks and tries to take us by storm.

Ignatius Loyola

It is a mark of the evil spirit to take on the appearance of an angel of light. He begins by whispering thoughts that are suited to a devout soul, and ends by suggesting his own.

Ignatius Loyola

In anything that is for the service of our Lord, the Devil tries his arts, working under the guise of holiness.

Teresa of Avila

The soul that is united with God is feared by the Devil as though it were God Himself.

John of the Cross

Let the enemy rage at the gate, let him knock, let him push, let him cry, let him howl, let him do worse; we know for certain that he cannot enter save by the door of our consent.

Francis de Sales

Modern times are dominated by Satan, and will be more so in the future.

Maximillian Kolbe

DEVOTION

Devotion is a certain act of the will by which man gives himself promptly to the service of God.

Thomas Aquinas

Devotion is spiritual agility and liveliness, by means of which charity works in us, or we in her, with love and readiness; and as charity leads us to obey and fulfill all God's commandments, so devotion leads us to obey them promptly and diligently.

Francis de Sales

Charity is a spiritual fire which, when it flames brightly, becomes devotion.

Francis de Sales

The ostrich never flies, the chicken flies but seldom, and then heavily and near the ground; but the swallow, the dove, and the eagle are ever on the wing; they fly far and easily. Even so sinners don't rise to God, but always grovel on the earth in pursuing earthly things. Well-meaning people who are as yet not truly devout mount up to God in good works, but rarely, slowly, and heavily. But the devout fly to Him perpetually, soaring lightly.

Francis de Sales

If charity is milk, devotion is the cream; if charity is a plant, devotion is the flower; if charity is a precious stone, devotion is its brilliance; if charity is a costly balsam, devotion is its fragrance, an odor of sweetness, that consoles men and makes the angels rejoice.

Francis de Sales

DISCRETION

One man carries an ax all his life and never cuts down a tree. Another, who knows how to cut, gives a few swings and the tree is down. This ax is discretion.

Ammonas the Hermit

Some wear down their bodies by fasting. But because they have no discretion, it puts them further from God.

Antony the Great

Without discretion, virtue becomes vice, and the natural impulses serve only to upset and wreck the personality.

Bernard of Clairvaux

Virtues demand discretion, and all excess is vice.

Bede the Venerable

Our body is not made of iron. Our strength is not that of stone. Live and hope in the Lord, and let your service be according to reason.

Clare of Assisi

DISSENT, DISSIDENTS— *See Heresy, Heretics*

THE DIVINIZATION OF THE SAINTS

He became man so that we might be made God.

Athanasius of Alexandria

For you He entered time, so that you might become eternal.

Augustine of Hippo

For men are not gods by being so in themselves, but they become gods by participation in that one God who is the true God.

Augustine of Hippo

God is what we ourselves aspired to be when we fell away from Him, when we listened to the voice of the seducer—"You shall be as gods"—and thus abandoned the very One who intended to make us gods, not by our desertion of Him, but by our participation in Him.

Augustine of Hippo

The proper effect of the Eucharist is the transformation of man into God.

Thomas Aquinas

By virtue of love is the lover transformed in the beloved and the beloved is transformed in the lover. Just as hard iron in the forge takes on the color, heat, energy, and form of the fire to such a degree that it almost turns into fire, so the soul, united with God through the perfect grace of divine love, will itself become almost divine and transformed in God.

Angela of Foligno

DOCTRINE

The knowledge of doctrines is a precious possession.

Cyril of Jerusalem

Church doctrines are a powerful weapon; they were not sent into the world for nothing. God's word does not return to Him void.

John Henry Cardinal Newman

DOCTRINE, DEVELOPMENT OF

If a divine gift has made you suitable in genius and experience to be in doctrine the [adorner] of the spiritual tabernacle, cut out the precious gems of divine dogma, shape them faithfully, ornament them wisely, add splendor, grace, and beauty to them! By your expounding it, may that now be understood more clearly what was formerly believed in its obscurity.

Vincent of Lerins

Regarding its substance, faith does not grow with the passage of time, for whatever has been believed since the beginning was contained in the faith of the ancient fathers. As regards its explication, however, the number of articles has increased, for we moderns explicitly believe what they believed implicitly.

Thomas Aquinas

From the nature of the human mind, time is necessary for the full comprehension and perfection of great ideas.

John Henry Cardinal Newman

DOGMA

The Church of Christ, zealous and cautious guardian of the dogmas deposited with it, never changes any phrase of them. It does not diminish them or add to them; it neither trims what seems necessary nor grafts things superfluous; it neither gives up its own nor usurps what does not belong to it. But it devotes all its diligence to one aim: to treat tradition faithfully and wisely; to nurse and polish what from ancient times may have remained unshaped and unfinished; to consolidate and strengthen what was already clear and plain; and to guard what already was confirmed and defined.

Vincent of Lerins

From the age of fifteen, dogma has been the fundamental principle of my religion. I know of no other religion; I cannot enter into the idea of any other sort of religion; religion, as a mere sentiment, is to me a dream and a mockery.

John Henry Cardinal Newman

Religion cannot but be dogmatic; it ever has been. All religions have had doctrines; all have professed to carry with them benefits which could be enjoyed only on condition of believing the word of a supernatural informant, that is, of embracing some doctrines or other.

John Henry Cardinal Newman

No doctrine is defined until it is violated.

John Henry Cardinal Newman

DOUBT

The disbelief of Thomas has done more for our faith than the faith of the other disciples. As he touches Christ and is won over to belief, every doubt is cast aside and our faith is strengthened.

Pope Gregory the Great

A thousand difficulties do not make a single doubt.

John Henry Cardinal Newman

DRESS

The dress of the body should not discredit the good of the soul.

Cyprian of Carthage

If you style your hair sumptuously, and walk so as to draw attention in public, and attract the eyes of youth upon you, and draw the sighs of young men after you, nourishing the lust of concupiscence and inflaming the fuel of sighs—so that, although you yourself aren't corrupted, yet you corrupt others, and offer yourself like a sword or poison to those who see you—you can't be excused on the pretense that you're chaste and modest in mind. Your shameful dress and immodest ornament accuse you: ... You're living in such a manner as to make yourselves objects of desire.

Cyprian of Carthage

The purpose of clothing is to keep warm in winter and to cover your nakedness, not to serve your vanity.

Cyril of Jerusalem

To change your disposition is a much greater accomplishment than to change your dress.

Jerome

Silk and purple and rouge and paint have beauty, but they do not impart it…. The beauty that is put on with a garment and is put off with the garment belongs without a doubt to the garment, and not to the wearer of it.

Bernard of Clairvaux

How proud is many a man who looks down on his neighbor because the wool of his gown is finer! Yet as fine as it is, a poor sheep wore it upon her back before it came upon his back, and all the while she wore it, she was after all still only a sheep. And why should he now think himself better than she was simply by having that wool—wool that, even though it is now his, is still not so truly his as it was truly hers?

Thomas More

DRUNKENNESS

Drunkenness is the ruin of reason. It is premature old age. It is temporary death.

Basil the Great

The drunken man is a living corpse.

John Chrysostom

Wine is for mirth, not for madness.

John Chrysostom

DUTIES, DUTY

In doing what we ought, we deserve no praise, because it is our duty.

Augustine of Hippo

Each state of life has its special duties; by accomplishing them, one may find happiness.

Nicholas of Flue

Never think yourself safe because you do your duty in ninety-nine points; it is the hundredth which is to be the ground of your self-denial.

John Henry Cardinal Newman

God has given me one grace—I'm not afraid of a fight; I have to do my duty, come what may.

Thérèse of Lisieux

EASTER

Earth her joy confesses, clothing her for spring;
All fresh gifts returned with her returning King.
Blooms in every meadow, leaves on every bow,
Speak His sorrow ended, hail His triumph now:
"Welcome, happy morning!" age to age shall say.

Venantius Fortunatus

'Tis the spring of souls today: Christ hath burst His prison;
And from three days' sleep in death as a Sun hath risen.
All the winter of our sins, long and dark, is flying
From His light, to whom we give laud and praise undying.
Now the queen of seasons, bright with the day of splendor,
With the royal feast of feasts comes its joy to render!

John of Damascus

Now let the heavens be joyful; let earth her song begin;
Let the round world keep triumph, and all that is therein!
Let all things seen and unseen their notes of gladness blend,
For Christ the Lord hath risen, our Joy that hath no end!

John of Damascus

EDUCATION, LEARNING — *See also Knowledge*

Truly barren is a secular education. It is always in labor, but never gives birth.

Gregory of Nyssa

What is nobler than to rule minds or to mold the character of the young? I consider that he who knows how to form the youthful mind is truly greater than all painters, sculptors, and all others of that sort.

John Chrysostom

He who is educated and eloquent must not measure his saintliness merely by his fluency. Of two imperfect things, holy rusticity is better than sinful eloquence.

Jerome

Free curiosity is of more value in learning than harsh discipline.

Augustine of Hippo

Anyone who wants to practice perfect poverty must renounce all worldly wisdom and even secular learning, to a certain extent. Divested of these possessions, he will be able to make the great acts of God his theme and offer himself naked to the embrace of the Crucified. Anyone who clings to his own opinions in the depths of his heart has not renounced the world perfectly.

Francis of Assisi

I would rather have learning joined with virtue than all the treasures of kings.

Thomas More

Untilled ground, however rich, will bring forth thistles and thorns; so also the mind of man.

Teresa of Avila

Religious truth is not only a portion, but a condition of general knowledge. To blot it out is nothing short, if I may so speak, of unraveling the web of university teaching.

John Henry Cardinal Newman

ENEMIES

May I be no man's enemy, and may I be the friend of that which is eternal and abides.

Eusebius of Vercelli

Let us learn to feel for the ills our neighbors suffer, and we will learn to endure the ills they inflict.

John Chrysostom

You don't love in your enemies what they are, but what you would have them to become.

Augustine of Hippo

Just as fawning friends pervert us, so also quarrelsome enemies often correct us.

Augustine of Hippo

Every man is his own enemy.

Bernard of Clairvaux

A man truly loves his enemy when he is not offended by the injury done to himself, but for love of God feels burning sorrow for the sin his enemy has brought on his own soul, and proves his love in a practical way.

Francis of Assisi

Give me Your grace, good Lord ... to think my greatest enemies my best friends; for the brothers of Joseph could never have done him so much good with their love and favor as they did him with their malice and hatred.

Thomas More

We should love and feel compassion for those who oppose us, since they harm themselves and do us good, and adorn us with crowns of everlasting glory.

Anthony Mary Zaccaria

ENVY

Whenever you envy your neighbor, you give demons a place to rest.

Ephraem the Syrian

When a man envies his brother the good that God says or does through him, it is like committing a sin of blasphemy, because he is really envying God, who is the only source of every good.

Francis of Assisi

Such is the wretched appetite of this cursed envy: ready to run into the fire, so that he may draw his neighbor with him!

Thomas More

If we were to ... esteem everything according to its true nature, rather than according to men's false opinion, then we would never see any reason to envy any man, but rather we would pity every man—and pity those most who have the most to be envied for, since they are the ones who will shortly lose the most.

Thomas More

ETERNITY

How can you admire the heavens, my son, when you see that you are more permanent than they? For the heavens pass away, but you will abide for all eternity with Him who is forever.

Gregory of Nyssa

The present is nothing. But eternity abides for those on whom all truth, all good, has shone, in one entire and perfect Light.

Paulinus of Nola

Blessed be God, we shall find no changes of weather in eternity!

Teresa of Avila

Eternity, eternity, when shall I come to you at last?… Eternity, where we will love with a glance of the soul.

Elizabeth Ann Seton

Eternity, oh, how near it often seems to me. Think of it when you are hard pushed. How long will be that day without a night or that night without a day.

Elizabeth Ann Seton

We must often draw the comparison between time and eternity. This is the remedy of all our troubles. How small will the present moment appear when we enter that great ocean!

Elizabeth Ann Seton

Time is short, eternity is long.

John Henry Cardinal Newman

I travel, work, suffer my weak health, meet with a thousand difficulties, but all these are nothing, for this world is so small. To me, space is an imperceptible object, as I am accustomed to dwell in eternity.

Frances Xavier Cabrini

THE EUCHARIST—*See also Communion, Daily*

Break one loaf, which is the medicine of immortality, and the antidote that wards off death but yields continuous life in union with Jesus Christ.

Ignatius of Antioch

They hold aloof from the Eucharist and from services of prayer, because they do not confess that the Eucharist is the flesh of our Savior Jesus Christ, which suffered for our sins and which, in His goodness, the Father raised from the dead. Therefore, those who argue against the gift of God will die in their disputes.

Ignatius of Antioch

He Himself, therefore, having declared and said of the Bread, "This is My Body," who will dare any longer to doubt? And when He Himself has affirmed and said, "This is My Blood," who can ever hesitate and say it is not His Blood?

Cyril of Jerusalem

Do not, therefore, regard the bread and wine as simply that, for they are, according to the Master's declaration, the Body and Blood of Christ. Even though the senses suggest to you the other, let faith make you firm. Do not judge in this matter by taste, but be fully assured by faith, not doubting that you have been deemed worthy of the Body and Blood of Christ.

Cyril of Jerusalem

This fountain is a fountain of light, shedding abundant rays of truth. And beside it the powers from on high have taken their stand, gazing on the beauty of its streams, since they perceive more clearly than we the power of what lies before us and its unapproachable dazzling rays.

John Chrysostom

If you were to put your hand or tongue into molten gold—if that were possible—you would make your hand or tongue golden. In much the same way, the Mystery lying before us here affects the soul.

John Chrysostom

Here a spiritual well of fire gushes up out of this Table!

John Chrysostom

Let us return from that Table like lions breathing out fire, terrifying to the Devil!

John Chrysostom

To show the love He has for us, He has made it possible for those who desire it not merely to look upon Him, but even to touch Him and to consume Him and to fix their teeth in His flesh and to be commingled with Him—in short, to fulfill all their love.

John Chrysostom

How many these days say, "I wish I could see His form, His appearance, His garments, His sandals!" Only look! You see Him! You touch Him! You eat Him!

John Chrysostom

Just as if someone were to twist two pieces of wax together and melt them with a fire, so that the two are made one, so too through participation in the Body of Christ and in His precious Blood, He is united to us and we to Him. In no other way can our corruptible nature be made alive except by being united bodily to the Body of Him who is, by His very nature, Life: that is, the Only-Begotten.

Cyril of Alexandria

All those are damned who see the Sacrament of the Body of Christ on the altar in the form of bread and wine by the words of our Lord in the hands of the priest, yet do not see or believe in spirit and in God that this is really the most holy Body and Blood of our Lord Jesus Christ.

Francis of Assisi

Every day He humbles Himself just as He did when He came from His heavenly throne into the Virgin's womb; every day He comes to us and lets us see Him in lowliness, when He descends from the bosom of the Father into the hands of the priest at the altar.

Francis of Assisi

Here, Lord Jesus, You are both Shepherd and green Pasture.

Thomas Aquinas

As in the life of the body, after a man is born and becomes strong, he requires food so that his life may be preserved and sustained, so also in the spiritual life, after being fortified, he requires spiritual food, which is

Christ's Body: Unless you shall eat of the flesh of the Son of Man, and drink of His Blood, you shall not have life in you.

Thomas Aquinas

Godhead here in hiding whom I do adore
Masked by these bare shadows, shape and nothing more;
See, Lord, at Thy service low here lies a heart
Lost, all lost in wonder at the God Thou art!

Thomas Aquinas

In every way that the soul can desire to feed, she will find in the Most Holy Sacrament sweetness and consolation.... Do you think that this most holy food isn't nourishment for these bodies, and an excellent remedy even against bodily ailments?... If when He lived in this world, He healed the sick by the mere touch of His garments, what doubt is there but that He will perform miracles, since He is so intimately within us, if we have a lively faith; and that He will grant us what we ask of Him, while He is in our house?

Teresa of Avila

On seeing the Blessed Sacrament when it was brought to his sickbed:
Here is my Love! Give Him to me quickly!

Philip Neri

Without the Holy Eucharist there would be no happiness in this world, and life wouldn't be bearable.

John Vianney

The man who communicates loses himself in God like a drop of water in the ocean: it's impossible to separate them anymore.... In these vast depths of love, there's enough to lose yourself for eternity.

John Vianney

There's nothing so great, my children, as the Eucharist. If you were to put all the good actions in the world against a Communion well made, it would be like a grain of dust against a mountain.

John Vianney

To someone who denied the doctrine of transubstantiation:
Jesus Christ said over the consecrated elements, "This is My Body." You say, "No. It is not His Body!" Whom am I to believe? I prefer to believe Jesus Christ.

Dominic Barberi

Yesterday, on approaching the Most Blessed Sacrament, I felt myself burning so violently that I felt obliged to move away. I was burning all over; it rose even to my face. Living Jesus! I am astonished that so many who receive Jesus are not reduced to ashes.

Gemma Galgani

Henceforth my motto shall be: "Give me the Eucharist, or let me die!"

Peter Julian Eymard

The Eucharist is the sun of the feasts of the Church. It sheds light on those feasts and renders them living and joyous.

Peter Julian Eymard

The Eucharist is the work of a measureless love that has at its service an infinite power, the omnipotence of God.

Peter Julian Eymard

Holy Communion is the shortest and safest way to heaven. There are others: innocence, but that is for little children; penance, but we are afraid of it; generous endurance for the trials of life, but when they come we weep and ask to be spared. The surest, easiest, shortest way is the Eucharist.

Pope Pius X

God being goodness itself—and goodness, in the language of Scripture, is the same as perfection—the Christian who is united to Jesus Christ in the Holy Eucharist finds in the efficacy of this sacrament all manner of perfection and holiness. From it he draws strength to rise above himself, to seek after eternal joys, and to despise the deceitful goods of this world because they are unable to satisfy his desires.

Pope Pius X

Since God is unsullied purity, he who is united to Jesus Christ in Holy Communion, rising like an innocent dove above the muddy water of this wretched world, wings his flight upward and seeks refuge in the bosom of God—the bosom of Him who is purer than the spotless snow that crowns the mountain tops.

Pope Pius X

EVIL

Do you know that often a root has split a rock when allowed to remain in it? Give no place to the seed of evil, seeing that it will break up your faith.

Cyril of Jerusalem

What is that which is called evil, except the lack of good?... For corruption is nothing but the destruction of good. Evil things therefore had their origin in good things, and unless they reside in good things, they do not exist at all.

Augustine of Hippo

God has deemed it better to bring good out of evil than not to permit evil at all.

Augustine of Hippo

Highest Providence often works a wonderful miracle: that of having evil men make others who are evil to become good.

Severinus

Take away all evil, and much good would go with it. God's care is to bring good out of the evils that happen, not to abolish them.

Thomas Aquinas

EXAMINATION OF CONSCIENCE

There are five points in this method of making the general examination of conscience. First, give thanks to God for favors received. Second, ask for grace to know my sins and to rid myself of them. Third, demand an account of my soul from the time of rising to the present examination. I should go over one hour after another, one period after another. The thoughts should be examined first, then the words, and finally the deeds....

Fourth, ask pardon of God our Lord for my faults. Fifth, resolve to amend with the grace of God. Close with an Our Father.

Ignatius Loyola

Before going to bed make a general examination of conscience, then ... go to sleep with a good thought in your mind.

Vincent de Paul

EXTREME UNCTION

In this life man encounters many obstacles that prevent him from being perfectly cleansed from his sins. And since no one can enter eternal life unless he is entirely cleansed from sin, another sacrament was needed whereby a man is cleansed from sin, delivered from his weakness, and prepared to enter the heavenly kingdom. This is the sacrament of Extreme Unction.

Thomas Aquinas

Extreme Unction ... does not always restore the health of the body ... because it may be that a man's life is not expedient for the salvation of his soul.

Thomas Aquinas

FAILURE

So you have failed?... You have not failed; you have gained experience. Forward!

Josemaria Escriva

FAITH

Faith is the ear of the soul.

Clement of Alexandria

God does not ask for our blood, but for our faith.

Cyprian of Carthage

We must neither doubt nor hesitate with respect to the words of the Lord; rather, we must be fully persuaded that every word of God is true and possible, even if our nature should rebel against the idea—for in this lies the test of faith.

Basil the Great

Whoever does not trust the Lord in small matters is quite clearly an unbe-
liever in things of greater importance.

Basil the Great

Faith means battles. If there are no contests, it is because there are none
who desire to contend.

Ambrose of Milan

It is good that faith should precede reason, lest we seem to demand reasons
from our Lord God in the same way that we might demand them of a
man. How unworthy it would be to believe the human testimonies of
another, and not believe the utterances of God Himself!

Ambrose of Milan

Without faith, every human labor is empty.

Fulgence of Ruspe

Faith is the proof of what cannot be seen. What is seen gives knowledge,
not faith.

Pope Gregory the Great

Faith furnishes prayer with wings, without which it cannot soar to heaven.

John Climacus

Faith is a sure foretaste, by the exercise of the will, of truth that is not yet
manifested.

Bernard of Clairvaux

By faith the Christian soul enters ... into marriage with God.

Thomas Aquinas

Faith is the foretaste of that knowledge which hereafter will make us happy.

Thomas Aquinas

Someone may object that it is foolish to believe what he cannot see.... Yet
life in this world would be altogether impossible if we were to believe only
what we can see. How can we live without believing others? How is a man
to believe that his father is So-and-so? Hence man finds it necessary to
believe others in matters that he cannot know perfectly on his own.

Thomas Aquinas

A faint faith is better than a strong heresy.

Thomas More

I trust you will be more reasonable than was one man in his attitude toward a liar. He swore that he would not, even for twenty coins, listen to that liar say his Creed. For he knew the man to be so untruthful that he thought he would no longer believe his own Creed if he heard it once out of the mouth of this liar.

Thomas More

Only a person of very small faith could believe that so great a God doesn't have the power to give food to those who serve Him.

Teresa of Avila

Faith is the union of God with the soul.

John of the Cross

It is because of faith that we exchange the present for the future.

Fidelis of Sigmaringen

Faith is ... a beam radiating from the face of God.

John Eudes

I may love by halves, I may obey by halves; I cannot believe by halves: either I have faith, or I have it not.

John Henry Cardinal Newman

What is more elevating and transporting, than the generosity of heart that risks everything on God's word.

John Henry Cardinal Newman

FAITH AND LOVE

Have a steadfast faith in Jesus Christ and love Him. That is the beginning and end of life: faith the beginning and love the end. When the two are united you have God. Everything else that has to do with real goodness is dependent on faith and love.

Ignatius of Antioch

Let no one be puffed up by his rank, for faith and love are everything, and nothing is more precious than these.

Ignatius of Antioch

Just as the mere memory of fire doesn't warm the body, so also faith without love doesn't produce the light of knowledge in the soul.

Maximus the Confessor

FAITH AND WORKS

How can a man say he believes in Christ if he doesn't do what Christ commanded him to do?

Cyprian of Carthage

True religion consists of these two elements: pious doctrines and virtuous actions. God does not accept doctrines apart from good works, nor are works, when divorced from godly doctrines, accepted by God. What does it profit a man to be an expert theologian if he is a shameless fornicator; or to be nobly self-controlled, but an impious blasphemer?

Cyril of Jerusalem

If we ask the question whether Jesus is the Christ, all who are Christians reply yes with one voice. But let their voices be silent for a little while so we can question their lives.

Augustine of Hippo

The mother of faith is hard work and an upright heart; the one builds up belief, the other makes it endure.

John Climacus

When men are slow to do good, they fast lose both faith and grace. For we find far more men who would rather believe well than do well.

Thomas More

Much caution is necessary, lest by much talk about faith, and much insistence on it without any distinctions or explanations, occasion be given to the people, whether before or after they have faith informed by charity, to become slothful and lazy in good works.

Ignatius Loyola

FAITH, HOPE, AND LOVE (CHARITY)

Love ... the Apostle Paul declares to be greater than the other two graces, that is, than faith and hope.... For when there is a question as to whether a man is good, we don't ask what he believes, or what he hopes, but what he loves.

Augustine of Hippo

There is no love without hope, no hope without love, and neither love nor hope without faith.

Augustine of Hippo

All things are possible for him who believes, more to him who hopes, even more to him who loves.

Lawrence of Brindisi

O man, believe in God with all your might, for hope rests on faith, love on hope, and victory on love; the reward will follow victory, the crown of life the reward, but the crown is the essence of things eternal.

Nicholas of Flue

My children, the three acts of faith, hope, and charity contain all the happiness of man upon earth.

John Vianney

THE FAMILY — *See also Children; Marriage*

We take care of our possessions for our children, but the children themselves we take no care of at all. What an absurdity this is! Form the soul of the son aright, and all the rest will be added afterward.

John Chrysostom

Isn't it absurd to send children out to jobs and to school, and to do all you can to prepare them for these, and yet not to "bring them up in the chastening and admonition of the Lord" [Eph. 6:4]?... Discipline is needed, not eloquence; character, not cleverness; deeds, not words. These gain a man the kingdom.

John Chrysostom

Disorder in the society is the result of disorder in the family.

Angela Merici

Love no child of your own so tenderly that you would not be content to sacrifice him to God as Abraham was ready to do for Isaac, if God were to command you to do so. And since we know that God would never do that, offer your child otherwise to God's service.

Thomas More

Depart, accursed fathers and mothers! Depart into the hell where the wrath of God awaits you, you and the good deeds you have done, while all the time you have let your children run wild. Depart into hell; they will not be long in joining you there.

John Vianney

For many years I have had no prayer for my children but that our Blessed God would do everything to them and in them in the way of affliction and adversity, if only—He will save their souls!

Elizabeth Ann Seton

Happiness is to be found only in the home where God is loved and honored, where each one loves, and helps, and cares for the others.

Theophane Venard

My last desire, children, is that the love of our Lord dwell in you so that it will change you into so many apostles, zealous for His glory. You will be the treasure of your families, whom you will make happy by your good conduct.

Pope Pius X

FASTING AND ABSTINENCE

How do we distinguish the fasting of our God and King from the fasting of that tyrant the Devil? Clearly by its moderation.... Everything that is extreme is destructive.

Amma Syncletice

Fasting is a medicine.

John Chrysostom

The immoderate long fasts of many displease me, for I have learned by experience that the donkey worn out with fatigue on the road seeks rest at any cost. In a long journey, strength must be supported.

Jerome

Total abstinence is easier than perfect moderation.

Augustine of Hippo

I abstain from flesh lest I should cherish the vices of the flesh. A man becomes a beast by loving what beasts love.

Bernard of Clairvaux

Don't you know that fasting can master concupiscence, lift up the soul, confirm it in the paths of virtue, and prepare a fine reward for the Christian?

Hedwig of Silesia

Abstinence is the mother of health. A few ounces of going without is an excellent recipe for any ailment.

Anthony Grassi

Continual moderation is better than fits of abstinence interspersed with occasional excesses.

Francis de Sales

As long as he who fasts, fasts for God, and he who fasts not, also fasts not for God, devotion is as well satisfied with one as with the other.

Francis de Sales

They alone can truly feast, who have first fasted.

John Henry Cardinal Newman

FAULT-FINDING

We are too fond of flinging our own faults behind our backs, so that we may fix all our attention on the foibles and failings of others.

Pior

Would to God that we were all of the mind to think that no man is as bad as ourselves! For that would be the way to mend both them and ourselves. But as it is now, they blame us, and we blame them, though both sides are actually worthy of blame, and both are more ready to find others' faults than they are to correct their own.

Thomas More

We would all much better mend our ways if we were as ready to pray for one another as we are to offer one another reproach and rebuke.

Thomas More

Let us look at our own shortcomings and leave other people's alone; for those who live carefully ordered lives are apt to be shocked at everything, and we might well learn very important lessons from the persons who shock us.

Teresa of Avila

Nothing would be done at all, if a man waited until he could do it so well that no one could find fault with it.

John Henry Cardinal Newman

FEAR

When we say, "Deliver us from evil," there remains nothing further that ought to be asked. For once we have asked God's protection against evil, and have obtained it, then we stand secure and safe against everything that the Devil and the world would work against us. What fear is there in this life for the one whose guardian in this life is God?

Cyprian of Carthage

The weight of fear is the anchor of the heart.

Pope Gregory the Great

Ah, fear, abortive imp of drooping mind; self-overthrow, false friend, root of remorse … ague of valor … love's frost, the mint of lies.

Robert Southwell

We must not fear fear.

Francis de Sales

What has a person to fear who lives in the arms and bosom of God?

Paul of the Cross

FEAR OF GOD

No one in all creation is rich but the one who fears God.

Ephraem the Syrian

The fear of God prepares a place for love. But once love has begun to dwell in our hearts, the fear that prepared the place for it is driven out.... In sewing, the needle introduces the thread into the cloth. The needle goes in, but the thread cannot follow unless the needle comes out first. In the same way, the fear of God first occupies our minds, but it does not remain there, because it enters only in order to introduce love.

Augustine of Hippo

The fear of God wounds us like a surgeon's knife.

Augustine of Hippo

Perfect love ... leads a man on to perfect fear. Such a man fears and keeps to God's will, not for fear of punishment, not to avoid condemnation, but ... because he has tasted the sweetness of being with God; he fears he may fall away from it.

Dorotheos of Gaza

I have learned for a fact that nothing so effectively obtains, retains, and regains grace, as that we should always be found not high-minded before God, but filled with holy fear.

Bernard of Clairvaux

Though the zealous service of God our Lord out of pure love should be esteemed above all, we should also praise highly the fear of the Divine Majesty. For not only the fear of a son, but also the fear of a slave, is pious and very holy. When nothing higher or more useful is attained, the fear of a slave is very helpful for rising from mortal sin, and once this is accomplished, one may easily advance to the fear of a son, which is wholly pleasing and agreeable to God our Lord since it is inseparably associated with the love of Him.

Ignatius Loyola

Perfect charity casts out fear, that is, the fear of pain, not the fear of fault—for true servants of God are always fearful of offending the Supreme Good, and this is indeed the holy fear of God.

Paul of the Cross

THE FLESH

Love the knowledge of the Scriptures and you will not love the errors of the flesh.

Jerome

We who are slaves of Christ make our bodies serve and our minds govern, so that the flesh receives its orders and accompanies our will, which is guided by Christ our Maker.

Paulinus of Nola

Inordinate love of the flesh is cruelty, because under the appearance of pleasing the body, we kill the soul.

Bernard of Clairvaux

FOLLY, HOLY

We were deceived by the wisdom of the serpent, but we are freed by the foolishness of God.

Augustine of Hippo

The virtue of innocence is held as foolishness by the wise of this world. Anything that is done out of innocence, they doubtless consider to be stupidity, and whatever truth approves of, in practice is called folly by men of worldly wisdom.

Pope Gregory the Great

What else do worldlings think we're doing but playing around when we flee what they most desire on earth, and desire what they flee? We're like jesters and tumblers who, with heads down and feet in the air, draw all eyes to themselves.

Bernard of Clairvaux

Out of gratitude and love for Him, we should desire to be reckoned fools and glory in wearing his costume.

Ignatius Loyola

To be a saint, you must be beside yourself. You must lose your head.

John Vianney

FOOD AND DRINK

It is fitting before we partake of food to bless the Maker of all things, and to sing when we drink.

Clement of Alexandria

One ought to arise from a meal able to apply oneself to prayer and study.

Jerome

In comparison with the stars, what is more trifling a matter than my dinner?

Augustine of Hippo

Take even bread with moderation, lest an overloaded stomach make you weary of prayer.

Bernard of Clairvaux

Food ought to be a refreshment to the body, and not a burden.

Bonaventure

The success of your morning meditation will largely depend on what you have eaten the night before.

Alphonsus Liguori

Have a good appetite. God does not want His spouses to look as though He fed them on lizards.

Raphaela Maria Porras

FORGIVENESS

No one heals himself by wounding another.

Ambrose of Milan

There are many kinds of alms the giving of which helps us to obtain pardon for our sins; but none is greater than that by which we forgive from our heart a sin that someone has committed against us.

Augustine of Hippo

The saints rejoiced at injuries and persecutions, because in forgiving them they had something to present to God when they prayed to Him.

Teresa of Avila

FREE WILL

The freedom of the will is then true freedom when it does not serve vices and sins.

Augustine of Hippo

Grace is necessary to salvation, free will is equally so; but grace in order to give salvation, free will in order to receive it.

Bernard of Clairvaux

Take away free will, and there remains nothing left to save…. Salvation is given by God alone, and it is given only to the free will. Even as it cannot be wrought without the consent of the receiver, it cannot be wrought without the grace of the Giver.

Bernard of Clairvaux

God presses us, but does not oppress our liberty.

Francis de Sales

FREEDOM, LIBERTY

Yoke yourself under the law of God, so that you may be in truth a free man.

Ephraem the Syrian

The chains of grace are so powerful, and yet so sweet, that though they attract our heart, they do not shackle our freedoms.

Francis de Sales

I leave you the spirit of liberty—not that which excludes obedience, for that is the liberty of the flesh; but that which excludes restraint, scruple, and worry.

Frances de Sales

FREEDOM OF RELIGION

When threatened with the choice between martyrdom or worship of the Roman gods:

That piety is worthless which forces men to be crushed against their will.

Crispina of Thacora

You can force a man to enter a church, to approach the altar, to receive the Sacrament; but you cannot force him to believe.

Augustine of Hippo

Unbelievers who have never accepted the faith should be subjected to no compulsion at all, for belief is an act of freedom. Given the power, however, the faithful may use force to prevent unbelievers from impeding the faith by blasphemy, or evil persuasion, or open persecution.

Thomas Aquinas

FRIENDS, FRIENDSHIP

Speaking of his dear friend St. Gregory Nazianzen:
We lived in each other.

Basil the Great

For in this way especially does a friend differ from a flatterer: The flatterer speaks to give pleasure, but the friend refrains from nothing, even that which causes pain.

Basil the Great

True friendship can harbor no suspicion; a friend must speak to a friend as freely as to his second self.

Jerome

There is no true friendship, Lord, except between those whom You bind together.... If your delight is in souls, my friends, let them be loved in God, for they too are changeable, and they will perish and pass away if they are not firmly established in Him. In Him, then, let them be loved; and draw to Him along with you as many souls as you can.

Augustine of Hippo

Blessed are those who love You, Lord, and their friends in You. For they are the only ones who will never lose anyone dear to them, since all who are dear to them are in You, our God, who can never be lost.

Augustine of Hippo

My soul and his soul were but one soul in two bodies.

Augustine of Hippo

Whether you like it or not, you will always grow apart from other human beings. But Christ is faithful and will always be with you.

John of God

What a great favor God does to those whom He places in the company of good people!

Teresa of Avila

If the bond of your communion is love, devotion, and Christian perfection, then your friendship will be precious indeed: precious because it has its origin in God, because it is maintained in God, and because it will endure forever in Him.

Francis de Sales

It is a kind of death to leave a place where one is well known and has friends.

Claude de la Colombiere

The accidents of life separate us from our dearest friends, but let us not despair. God is like a looking glass in which souls see each other. The more we are united to Him by love, the nearer we are to those who belong to Him.

Elizabeth Ann Seton

FRIENDSHIP WITH GOD

Intimacy with the Lord is not a matter of physical kinship; rather, it is achieved by cheerful readiness to do the will of God.

Basil the Great

True perfection consists in having but one fear: the fear of losing God's friendship.

Gregory of Nyssa

We regard falling from God's friendship as the only thing to be feared and we consider becoming God's friend the only thing worthy of honor and desire.

Pope Gregory the Great

Mental prayer is nothing else ... but being on terms of friendship with God, frequently conversing in secret with Him.

Teresa of Avila

A prayer said after a cart in which she was riding overturned on a journey to found a Carmelite convent:
No wonder You have so few friends, since this is the way You treat them!

Teresa of Avila

Take God for your Spouse and Friend and walk with Him continually, and you will not sin and will learn to love, and the things you must do will work out prosperously for you.

John of the Cross

The Cross is the gift God makes to His friends.

John Vianney

I have such a marvelous friend. I make myself content with God when I am not content with myself.

Miguel of Ecuador

Be not like those who are before [God] like a slave, and wait the end of their duty of obligation to find their liberty and pleasure in leaving Him.

Elizabeth Ann Seton

GAMBLING
The Devil invented gambling.

Augustine of Hippo

GENTLENESS
Nothing is so strong as gentleness, nothing so gentle as real strength.

Francis de Sales

I have never succeeded when I have spoken with the faintest suspicion of hardness. One must be ever on one's guard not to embitter the heart, if one wishes to move the mind.

Vincent de Paul

GIFTS, GIVING

Small vessels may hold great gifts.

Ephraem the Syrian

I do not lend. I give. Hasn't the good God been the first to give to me?

John Vianney

GLUTTONY

If a king wants to take a city whose citizens are hostile, he first captures their food and water, and when they are starving he subdues them. So it is with gluttony. If a man is earnest in fasting and making himself hungry, the enemies that trouble his soul will grow weak.

John the Short

The necessity [of eating and drinking] is sweet to me, and against this sweetness must I fight, so that I might not be made captive by it.... This much You have taught me: that I must look upon food as medicine.

Augustine of Hippo

Gluttony is hypocrisy of the stomach. Filled, it moans that there isn't enough; stuffed and crammed, it wails that it's still hungry. Gluttony thinks up seasonings, creates sweet recipes. Stop one urge, and out bursts another.

John Climacus

It is impossible to engage in spiritual conflict unless the appetite has first been subdued.

Pope Gregory the Great

Irrational feeding darkens the soul and makes it unfit for spiritual experiences.

Thomas Aquinas

If we see men die from famine in some year of scarcity, we consider it a serious matter.... But in times of abundance, every year there are many people who die of gluttony. Yet we take no heed of that at all, and we blame the sickness for the death it caused, rather than blaming gluttony for the sickness it caused.

Thomas More

If men would examine how many are killed with weapons and how many eat and drink themselves to death, there would be found more dead from the cup and the kitchen than from the thrust of a sword.

Thomas More

It is almost certain that excess in eating is the cause of almost all the diseases of the body, but its effects on the soul are even more disastrous.

Alphonsus Liguori

Never rise from the table without having given due thanks to the Lord. If we act in this way, we need have no fear of the wretched sin of gluttony.

Padre Pio of Pietrelcina

GOD

Nothing is impossible to God except for lying.

Pope Clement I

God is not contained, but is Himself the place of everything.

Theophilus of Antioch

Ten thousand names would not suffice You!

Ephraem the Syrian

Of God, we cannot say all that ought to be said…. In those matters that concern God, to confess our ignorance is already great knowledge.

Cyril of Jerusalem

There is no one name sufficiently broad to take in the whole nature of God.

Basil the Great

To speak of the Godhead is, I know, like trying to cross the ocean on a raft, or trying to fly to the stars on a little bird's wings.

Gregory Nazianzen

God always was, and is, and will be; or better, He always *is:* "Was" and "will be" are portions of time as we reckon it, and are of a changing nature. He, however, is ever existing…. He gathers in Himself the whole of being, because He neither has beginning nor will He have an end. He is like some great Sea of Being, limitless and unbounded, transcending every conception of time and nature.

Gregory Nazianzen

We therefore call God Himself the indescribable, the unfathomable, the invisible, the incomprehensible, the One who surpasses the power of the human tongue, who exceeds the comprehension of the mortal mind, who is inscrutable even to the angels, who is unseen by the seraphim, who is unfathomable to the cherubim, who is invisible to principalities, powers, and virtues, and to every creature without exception, known by the Son alone and the Holy Spirit.

John Chrysostom

What is impossible to God? Not that which is difficult to His power, but that which is contrary to His nature.

Ambrose of Milan

For who is lord but our Lord? Or who is God besides our God? Most high, most excellent, most mighty, most omnipotent; most merciful and most just; most hidden and most near; most beautiful and most strong; constant, yet incomprehensible; unchangeable, yet changing all things; never new, never old; renewing all things, yet bringing old age upon the proud, without their knowing it; always working, yet always at rest; gathering, yet needing nothing; upholding, filling, and protecting; creating, nourishing, and perfecting; still seeking, though You lack nothing. You love, but are not agitated by Your love; You are jealous, yet free from care; You are angry, yet You remain tranquil.... Can anyone who speaks of You ever say enough?

Augustine of Hippo

God ... is loved, wittingly or unwittingly, by everything that is capable of loving.

Augustine of Hippo

God: whom no one loses, unless deceived; whom no one seeks, unless stirred up; whom no one finds, unless made pure.

Augustine of Hippo

God is all eye, because He sees all; all ear, because He hears all; all mouth, because He is all Word; all tongue, because He speaks all; all foot, because He is everywhere; all hand, because He operates everywhere; all arm, because He embraces all and governs all. And no matter what you say of Him, you will only be naming the doing of His works and the arrangement of His mysteries.

Gregory of Elvira

I bind to myself today God's power to pilot me, God's might to uphold me, God's wisdom to teach me, God's eye to watch over me, God's ear to hear me, God's Word to give me speech, God's hand to guide me, God's way to lie before me, God's shield to shelter me, God's host to secure me.

Patrick of Ireland

Almost everything said of God is unworthy, for the very reason that it is capable of being said.

Pope Gregory the Great

God is within all things, but not included by them; outside all things, but not excluded by them; above all things, but not beyond their reach.

Pope Gregory the Great

All-powerful, all-holy, most high and supreme God, sovereign good, all good, every good, You who alone are good ... to You we must refer all good always.

Francis of Assisi

You are a Fire that takes away the cold, illuminates the mind with its light, and causes me to know the truth.

Catherine of Siena

Any thought not centered on God is stolen from Him.

John of the Cross

He who desires nothing but God is rich and happy.

Alphonsus Liguori

The great majority of men use their own short-sighted ideas as a yardstick for measuring the divine omnipotence.

Thérèse of Lisieux

GOD AS FATHER

How great is the Lord's indulgence! How great is His condescension and abundant goodness toward us. Think of it: He has willed that we call Him Father when we come before Him to pray, and to call ourselves sons of God, even as Christ is the Son of God—a name that none of us would dare to use in prayer unless He Himself had allowed us to pray in that way!

Cyprian of Carthage

We ought then, beloved brothers, to remember and to know, that when we call God Father, we ought to act as God's children. Then, He can take as much pleasure in considering us His sons as we do in thinking of Him as our Father.

Cyprian of Carthage

The Father most tender, Father of all, my immense God—I His atom.

Elizabeth Ann Seton

GOD, THE BEAUTY OF

Glory to the Beautiful One, who conformed us to His image! Glory to the Fair One, who did not look upon our foulness!

Ephraem the Syrian

God is not dependent on anything for His beauty; His beauty is not limited to certain times or aspects; but He is beautiful by Himself, through Himself, and in Himself. He is eternal beauty—not changing from one moment to the next—constantly the same beyond all change or alteration, increase or addition.

Gregory of Nyssa

Blessed is the mind that, passing by all creatures, constantly rejoices in God's beauty.

Maximus the Confessor

If things created are so full of loveliness, how resplendent with beauty must be the One who made them! The wisdom of the Worker is apparent in His handiwork.

Anthony of Padua

In beautiful things Saint Francis saw Beauty Himself, and through His vestiges imprinted on creation he followed his Beloved everywhere, making from all things a ladder by which he could climb up and embrace Him who is utterly desirable.

Bonaventure

When once I had seen the great beauty of the Lord, I saw no one by comparison on whom my thoughts wished to dwell.

Teresa of Avila

God being infinite beauty, the soul united to Christ draws upon himself the admiring and tender gaze of the angels, who, were they capable of any passion, would be filled with envy at his lot.

Pope Pius X

GOD, THE LOVE OF

God loves each of us as if there were only one of us.

Augustine of Hippo

God's love for us is not greater in heaven than it is now.

Thomas Aquinas

There is no creature made who can realize how much, how sweetly, and how tenderly our Maker loves us. And therefore we can, with His grace and His help, stand in spirit, gazing with endless wonder at this lofty, immeasurable love—beyond human scope—that the Almighty, in His goodness, has for us.

Julian of Norwich

Eternal Beauty! ... You act as if You could not live without Your creature, even though You are Life itself, and everything has its life from You and nothing can live without You. Why then are you so mad? Because You have fallen madly in love with what You have made!

Catherine of Siena

When did God's love for you begin? When He began to be God. When did He begin to be God? Never, for He has always been without beginning and without end, and so He has always loved you from eternity.

Francis de Sales

He loves, He hopes, He waits. Our Lord prefers to wait Himself for the sinner for years rather than keep us waiting an instant.

Maria Goretti

GOD, THE PRESENCE OF

What world exists that could receive anyone who deserts Him?... Where can anyone go, where can he flee, to escape from Him who embraces everything?

Pope Clement I

Surely if we remembered that God sees us when we sin, we would never do what displeases Him.

Jerome

You, Lord, were within me, yet I was looking for You outside myself....
You were with me, but I was not with You.

Augustine of Hippo

When the Lord ascended into heaven, He departed from our sight, so that we might return to our own hearts and find Him there.

Augustine of Hippo

He is never absent, and yet He is far from the thoughts of the wicked; yet He is not absent when far away, for where He is not present by grace, He is present by vengeance.

Pope Gregory the Great

Realize above all that you are in God's presence ... empty yourself completely and sit waiting, content with the grace of God, like a chick that tastes nothing and eats nothing except what its mother gives it.

Romuald

In all our thoughts and actions we ought to remember the presence of God, and to count as lost any time in which we don't think of Him.

Bernard of Clairvaux

Always and everywhere, a person should aim to live as if God were visibly present.... Such alertness requires that we turn our minds fully and decisively to the Lord. The angels, wherever they may be sent, never stop gazing upon God. In the same way a virtuous person, as much as he can, always keeps the memory of God in his heart.

Bonaventure

Be assured that he who will always walk faithfully in God's presence, always ready to give Him an account of all his actions, will never be separated from Him by consenting to sin.

Thomas Aquinas

In two ways the presence of God is an antidote against sin: First, because God sees us, and second, because we see God.

Ignatius Loyola

Granting that we are always in the presence of God, yet it seems to me that those who pray are in His presence in a very different sense; for they, as it were, see that He is looking upon them, while others may go for days on end without even once recollecting that God sees them.

Teresa of Avila

We need no wings to go in search of Him, but have only to find a place where we can be alone—and look upon Him present within us.

Teresa of Avila

God dwells within you, and there you should dwell with Him.

Teresa of Avila

Lord, my God, You are not a stranger to Him who does not estrange himself from You. How do they say that it is You who absent Yourself?

John of the Cross

He is more within us than we are ourselves.

Elizabeth Ann Seton

Never make a decision without stopping to consider the matter in the presence of God.

Josemaria Escriva

GOD, THE WILL OF

"Thy will be done, on earth as it is in heaven." In this we pray, not that God should be able to do as He wills—for who can resist God to keep Him from doing as He wills? Rather, we pray that we may be able to do as God wills. Since we are hindered by the Devil from obeying with our thought and deed God's will in all things, we pray, asking that God's will may be done in us.

Cyprian of Carthage

The will of God is the measure of things.

Ambrose of Milan

For God, to will is to have done.

Jerome

The Creator has used the very will of the creature that was working in opposition to His will as an instrument for carrying out His will, the Supreme Good thus turning to good account even what is evil.... In a way unspeakably strange and wonderful, even what is done in opposition to His will does not defeat His will.

Augustine of Hippo

Therefore with mind entire, faith firm, courage undaunted, love thorough, let us be ready for whatever God wills.

Bede the Venerable

As in heaven Your will is punctually performed, so may it be done on earth by all creatures, particularly in me and by me.

Elizabeth of Hungary

The accomplishment of the divine will is the sole end for which we are in the world.

John Eudes

Feed upon the will of God and drink the chalice of Jesus with your eyes shut, so that you may not see what is inside.

Paul of the Cross

Do as vinedressers or gardeners whenever a storm threatens.... They run to a shelter and stay there in peace until the storm passes. That's what I want you to do with the grace of God. Always remain quiet and calm in the shelter of God's will, under the almighty protection of the Most High.

Paul of the Cross

Don't doubt but that God keeps you in His divine arms and that the time will come when He will teach you His most holy will.

Paul of the Cross

In every event of life, in all interior and exterior worries and desolations, in dryness, abandonment of spirit, physical sufferings, in all of these find the food of the divine will, and having found this divine good pleasure, take and eat all the hard and bitter morsels. Then, whether you are suffering or in joy, you will be able to rest in the bosom of the heavenly Father even though you are unable to see His face.

Paul of the Cross

Take the holy, gentle will of God as your spouse, wedded each moment by the ring of faith in which are set all the jewels of hope and love.

Paul of the Cross

If I want only pure water, what does it matter to me whether it be brought in a vase of gold or of glass? What is it to me whether the will of God be presented to me in tribulation or consolation, since I desire and seek only the divine will?

Francis de Sales

What was the first rule of our dear Savior's life?... To do His Father's Will.... Well, then, the first end I propose in our daily work is to do the Will of God; secondly, to do it in the manner He wills it; and thirdly, to do it because it is His Will.

Elizabeth Ann Seton

I will attempt day by day to break my will into little pieces. I want to do God's holy will, not my own.

Gabriel Possenti

If you really want to please God and intend to be in full agreement with His will, you can't go wrong.

Francis Libermann

GOOD WORKS

Each one, according to his own ability, should be a pattern of goodness to others.

Basil the Great

God is more pleased by one work, however small, done secretly, without desire that it be known, than a thousand done with desire that men know of them.

John of the Cross

He who does a pure and whole work for God merits a whole kingdom.

John of the Cross

A good work talked about is a good work spoiled.

Vincent de Paul

There is no greater error than to imagine that the very employments which God Himself gives us shall force us to forget Him while we are engaged in them.

Elizabeth Ann Seton

Do everything for the love of God and His glory without looking at the outcome of the undertaking. Work is judged, not by its result, but by its intention.

Padre Pio of Pietrelcina

THE GOSPEL

It is principally in the Gospel that the form of the Catholic faith and the rule of all Christian life is laid down.

Thomas Aquinas

Once glance at the holy Gospel, and the life of Jesus becomes a perfume that fills the very air I breathe.

Thérèse of Lisieux

GOSSIP

Don't let the tongue that has confessed Christ speak evil or cause disturbances; don't let it be heard clamoring with reproaches and quarrels; after its words of praise, don't let it spew snakes' venom against the brethren and the priests of God.

Cyprian of Carthage

Whenever you tell the shortcomings of someone who is not present, your tongue has made a harp for the music of the Devil.

Ephraem the Syrian

Go to church to pray, not to gossip.

Boniface of Mainz

We act like ravens and carrion crows who never bother with any living flesh—but wherever we may find a dead dog in a ditch, that's where we fly to stuff ourselves. In the same way, when we see a good man, and hear or see a good thing, then we take little heed. But when once we see an evil deed, then we stop and stare; and all day long we gossip and feed ourselves with the filthy delight of evil conversation.

Thomas More

Nothing should be said to lessen the good name of another, or to complain about him. For if I reveal the hidden mortal sin of another, I sin mortally; if I reveal a hidden venial sin, I sin venially; in his defect, I manifest my own.

Ignatius Loyola

Don't be curious about matters that don't concern you; never speak of them, and don't ask about them.

Teresa of Avila

Would we want our own hidden sins to be divulged? Then we should be silent about the hidden sins of others.

Jean Baptiste de la Salle

If something uncharitable is said in your presence, either speak in favor of the absent, or withdraw, or if possible stop the conversation.

John Vianney

GOTHIC ARCHITECTURE

That style which, whatever be its origin, is called Gothic, is endowed with a profound and a commanding beauty, such as no other style possesses with which we are acquainted, and which probably the Church will not see surpassed till it attain to the celestial city.

John Henry Cardinal Newman

GRACE, DIVINE

However well you may run, however well you may wrestle, you still need Him who gives the crown.

Gregory Nazianzen

It is not enough for me that God has given me grace once, but He must give it always. I ask, that I may receive; and when I have received, I ask again. I am covetous of receiving God's bounty. He is never slow in giving, nor am I ever weary of receiving. The more I drink, the more thirsty I become.

Jerome

It is our part to seek, His to grant what we ask; ours to make a beginning, His to bring it to completion; ours to offer what we can, His to finish what we cannot.

Jerome

All my hope is found solely in Your exceeding great mercy. Grant what You command, and command what You will.

Augustine of Hippo

Don't regret what is past, and don't trust in your own righteousness.

Anthony of Padua

Man, blinded and bowed, sits in darkness and cannot see the light of heaven unless grace with righteousness comes to his aid.

Bonaventure

Grace is nothing else but a certain beginning of glory in us.

Thomas Aquinas

Grace has five effects in us: First, our soul is healed; second, we will good; third, we work effectively for it; fourth, we persevere; fifth, we break through to glory.

Thomas Aquinas

Grace is the light by which men see the way to walk out of sin; and grace is the staff without whose help no man is able to rise out of sin.

Thomas More

If a man lowers a rope into a well and pulls someone out who could not escape by himself, wouldn't it be true that the man in the well didn't climb out by his own power? And yet he still contributed something of his own to the process by hanging onto the rope and not letting it get away. The freedom of the will is like that: It can do nothing without grace. But when the divine goodness grants grace generously, the free will of a good man holds fast to it and cooperates with it properly.

Thomas More

Those who imagine they can attain to holiness by any wisdom or strength of their own will find themselves after many labors, and struggles, and weary efforts, only the farther from possessing it, and this in proportion to their certainty that they of themselves have gained it.

John of Avila

There is no one who during this mortal life can properly judge how far he is an obstacle and to what extent he resists the workings of God's grace in his soul.

Ignatius Loyola

Cast yourself into the arms of God and be very sure that if He wants anything of you, He will fit you for the work and give you strength.

Philip Neri

No matter what efforts I make, I cannot die to myself without His grace. I am like a frog which, no matter how high it leaps, always finishes up back in the mud. No matter how hard I try to escape from myself, I always come back to myself and my self-love. Draw me, then, O Lord, draw me after You; for unless You do, I cannot move even one step away from myself.

Dominic Barberi

Trying to do good to people without God's help is no easier than making the sun shine at midnight. You discover that you've got to abandon all your own preferences, your own bright ideas, and guide souls along the road our Lord has marked out for them. You mustn't coerce them into some path of your own choosing.

Thérèse of Lisieux

GREATNESS

For it is part of a truly great man not merely to be equal to great things, but also to make little things great by his own power.

Basil the Great

He who does not abide in his littleness loses his greatness.

Francis de Sales

Great acts take time.

John Henry Cardinal Newman

For so it is with all greatness, that, because it is great, it cannot be comprehended by ordinary minds at once; but time, and distance, and contemplation are necessary for its being recognized by beholders.

John Henry Cardinal Newman

HAPPINESS

He is truly happy who has all that he wishes to have, and wishes to have nothing that he ought not to wish.

Augustine of Hippo

Whoever possesses God is happy.

Augustine of Hippo

We must acknowledge that God is happiness itself.

Severinus

Since happiness is nothing else but the enjoyment of the Supreme Good, and the Supreme Good is above us, no one can be happy who does not rise above himself.

Bonaventure

Happiness is the natural life of man.

Thomas Aquinas

HASTE

The affairs of God are accomplished little by little and almost imperceptibly. The Spirit of God is neither violent nor hasty.

Vincent de Paul

God does not hasten His works. He does all things in their time.

Vincent de Paul

It is not expedient to wish to do everything all at once, or to think that all is lost if everybody else does not hurry along with us.

Vincent de Paul

HEALTH

Through intemperate living we drive ourselves to sickness, and then patch ourselves up with medicine; but with a sober diet and temperance we might have less need of remedies and keep ourselves in health.

Thomas More

Just as too great a care for bodily things is reprehensible, so reasonable care is to be commended to preserve health for the service of God.

Ignatius Loyola

God prefers your health, and your obedience, to your penances.

Teresa of Avila

Take care of your health, that it may serve you to serve God.

Francis de Sales

Health of body and mind is a great blessing, if we can bear it.

John Henry Cardinal Newman

THE HEART

Let us remember, then, that within us there is a palace of immense magnificence. The entire edifice is built of gold and precious stones.... Truly there is no building of such great beauty as a pure soul, filled with virtues; and the greater these virtues, the brighter these stones sparkle.... In this palace the great King lodges, who has been pleased to become your Guest, and ... He sits there on a throne of tremendous value: your *heart*.

Teresa of Avila

Give me a heart as big as the universe.

Frances Xavier Cabrini

The heart is rich when it is content, and it is content when its desires are set upon God.

Miguel of Ecuador

HEAVEN

Man is made for the contemplation of heaven, and is in truth a heavenly plant, intended to come to the knowledge of God.

Clement of Alexandria

We regard paradise as our country.... There, a great number of our dear ones is awaiting us, and a dense crowd of parents, brothers, children, is longing for us, already assured of their own safety, and still solicitous for our salvation. To attain to their presence and their embrace, what a gladness both for them and for us as well!

Cyprian of Carthage

What a pleasure is there in the heavenly kingdom, without fear of death; and how lofty and perpetual a happiness with eternal life! There the glorious company of the apostles—there the host of the rejoicing prophets—there the innumerable multitude of martyrs, crowned for the victory of their struggle and suffering—there the triumphant consecrated virgins, who subdued the lust of the flesh and of the body by the strength of their self-control—there are merciful men rewarded, who by feeding and helping the poor have done the works of righteousness—who, keeping the Lord's precepts, have transferred their earthly inheritance to the heavenly treasuries. To these, beloved brethren, let us hasten with an eager desire; let us crave quickly to be with them, and quickly to come to Christ.

Cyprian of Carthage

Just as the soul even now finds it impossible to desire unhappiness, so in heaven it shall be wholly impossible for it to desire sin.

Augustine of Hippo

Merely to love things above is already to mount on high.

Pope Gregory the Great

I have been made for heaven, and heaven for me.

Joseph Cafasso

Heaven is not divided by the number of those who reign, nor lessened by being shared, nor disturbed by its multitude, nor disordered by its inequality of ranks, nor changed by motion, nor measured by time.

Bonaventure

The pleasant companionship of all the blessed in heaven will be a companionship replete with delight. For each one will possess all good things together with the blessed, because they will love one another as themselves, and therefore will rejoice in the happiness of others' goods as well as their own. Consequently, the joy and gladness of one will be as great as the joy of all.

Thomas Aquinas

Jesus told me, "My heaven would not be complete without you."

Gertrude the Great

I don't put a penny's value on this life if only our Lord will give me a tiny corner in Paradise.

Camillus de Lellis

The world is only peopled in order to people heaven.

Francis de Sales

Our home is heaven. On earth we're like travelers staying at a hotel. When you're away, you're always thinking of going home.

John Vianney

When you awake in *that* world, you will find that nothing could tempt you to return to *this!*

Elizabeth Ann Seton

Heaven is at present out of sight, but in due time, as snow melts and discovers what it lay upon, so will this visible creation fade away before those greater splendors which are behind it.

John Henry Cardinal Newman

The country in which I live is not my native country; *that* lies elsewhere, and it must always be the center of my longings.

Thérèse of Lisieux

HELL, DAMNATION, THE DAMNED

It is better to be punished and cleansed now than to be sent to the torment to come, when it will be time for punishing only, and not for cleansing.

Gregory Nazianzen

To be lost out of the kingdom of God, to be an exile from the city of God, to be alienated from the life of God, to have no share in that great goodness that God has laid up for those who fear Him and has created for those who trust in Him, would be a punishment so great that, if it were eternal, no torments that we know of, continued through as many ages as man's imagination can conceive, could be compared with it.

Augustine of Hippo

It is in vain that some, indeed very many, moan about eternal punishment, and the perpetual, uninterrupted torments of the lost, and say they do not believe it will be so. Though they do not blatantly deny Holy Scripture, yet at the suggestion of their own feelings, they soften down everything that seems hard, and give a milder turn to statements that they think are designed to frighten rather than to be received as literally true.... But this perpetual death of the wicked, that is, their alienation from the life of God, will abide forever.

Augustine of Hippo

The damned will be as though always dying and never dead and never going to die. For this reason damnation is described as everlasting death, seeing that just as a dying man is in extreme pain, even so are they who are in hell.

Thomas Aquinas

The regret and anguish of the damned will be useless, for it will not be on account of any hatred for evil, but on account of grief over being punished.

Thomas Aquinas

A man buys hell here with so much pain, that he might have heaven with less than half the amount.

Thomas More

The damned are in the abyss of hell, as within a woeful city, where they suffer unspeakable torments in all their senses and members, because as they have employed all their senses and their members in sinning, so shall they suffer in each of them the punishment due to sin.

Francis de Sales

Hell is full of the talented, but heaven of the energetic.

Jane Frances de Chantal

Lord, I will put myself at hell's gate, so that I can stop anyone else from entering there.

Dominic Barberi

HELL, CHRIST'S DESCENT INTO

He descended to the regions beneath the earth, that from there also He might redeem the righteous. For tell me, would you wish for the living to enjoy His grace, and that too when most of them are unholy, and yet have those who from Adam onward had been long imprisoned not at last obtain deliverance? The prophet Isaiah announced with loud voice so many things concerning Him; wouldn't you want the King to descend and deliver His herald? David was there, and Samuel, and all the prophets, and John the Baptist himself.... Wouldn't you want Him to descend and deliver such men?

Cyril of Jerusalem

A man's triumph over another is complete when he not only conquers him in the open field but attacks him in his stronghold and deprives him of his kingdom and even of his dwelling-place. Now Christ had triumphed over the Devil and had conquered him on the cross.... Therefore, that His victory might be complete, it was His will to deprive the Devil of his throne and to imprison him in his own house, which is hell. For this reason He descended there, deprived the Devil of his own, bound him, and carried off his spoils.

Thomas Aquinas

HERESY, HERETICS

Some have a wicked and deceitful way of flaunting the Name about, while acting in a way unworthy of God. They are mad dogs that bite secretly. You must be on your guard against them, for it is hard to heal their bite.

Ignatius of Antioch

I urge you, therefore—not I, but the love of Jesus Christ—eat only Christian food. Keep away from strange fare, by which I mean heresy. For those people mix Jesus Christ with their teachings, speaking things unworthy of belief. It is as if they were giving a deadly poison mixed with sweetened wine, so that the unsuspecting victim readily accepts it and drinks his own death with fatal pleasure.

Ignatius of Antioch

They still call themselves Christians after abandoning the Gospel of Christ and the observance of His law; though walking in darkness they think they still enjoy the light. The Enemy flatters and deceives them ... he transforms himself into an angel of light, and primes his servants to act as if they were servants of righteousness; to call the night day, and damnation salvation; to teach presumption and call it hope, disbelief and call it faith, Anti-Christ under the name of Christ; so that by lies that appear to be truth, they sabotage the truth with trickery.

Cyprian of Carthage

Heresies have often arisen and still arise because of this: Perverted minds have no peace, and faithless dissidents will not maintain unity. But the Lord endures and allows these things, while we still have the opportunity to choose freely, so that as the discernment of truth is testing our hearts and minds, the sound faith of those who are approved may shine clearly.

Cyprian of Carthage

Even the heretics appear to have Christ, for none of them denies the name of Christ; yet anyone who does not confess all that pertains to Christ does in fact deny Christ.

Ambrose of Milan

These modern men, who have sprouted up overnight as "theologians" claiming to know everything ... fail to agree among themselves about the great dogmas of the Christian faith. Each of them, whoever he may be, claiming that he has the truth, vanquishes the rest—only to be vanquished by the rest in turn. But they are all alike in this way: They all oppose the Catholic faith, and they all are conquered by it.

Thomas More

They turn the antidote of Holy Scripture into poison.

Thomas More

Latitudinarians, while they profess charity towards all doctrines, nevertheless count it heresy to oppose the principle of latitude.

John Henry Cardinal Newman

HOLINESS — *See Sanctification, Sanctity, Holiness*

THE HOLY SPIRIT

The Holy Spirit longs to find the gates of our heart, so that He may enter in and dwell there, and sanctify it; and He goes round about to all the gates to see where He may enter.

Ephraem the Syrian

The Holy Spirit is a power most mighty, a Being divine and unsearchable; for He is living and intelligent, a sanctifying principle of all things made by God through Christ.

Cyril of Jerusalem

To each who receives the Spirit, it is as if he alone received Him; yet the grace the Spirit pours out is quite sufficient for the whole of mankind.

Basil the Great

Now what the soul is to the body of man, the Holy Spirit is in the body of Christ, which is the Church. The Holy Spirit does in the whole Church what the soul does in all the members of a single body.

Augustine of Hippo

The Holy Spirit gives wisdom against folly, understanding against dullness, counsel against rashness, fortitude against fears, knowledge against ignorance, piety against hardness of our heart, and fear against pride.

Pope Gregory the Great

"Love" can be used either as an essential name of the divine nature or as a personal name of a divine person—then it is the proper name of the Holy Spirit, as "Word" is the proper name of the Son.

Thomas Aquinas

O Holy Spirit, who gives grace where You will, come into me and ravish me to Yourself. The nature that You made, change with honeysweet gifts, that my soul, filled with delightful joy, may despise and cast away all the things of this world, that it may receive spiritual gifts, given by You, and going with joyful songs into infinite light may be all melted in holy love.

Richard Rolle

Holy Spirit, Spirit of truth, You are the Reward of the saints, the Comforter of souls, Light in the darkness, Riches to the poor, Treasure to lovers, Food for the hungry, Comfort to those who are wandering; to sum up, You are the One in whom all treasures are contained.

Mary Magdalene dei Pazzi

The Holy Spirit rests in the soul of the righteous just like the dove in her nest. He hatches good desires in a pure soul, as the dove hatches her young.

John Vianney

HONORS, WORLDLY

If you want to be glorified, despise glory.

John Chrysostom

The honors of this world—what are they but puff and emptiness and peril of falling?

Augustine of Hippo

The effort to please men clothes itself in the words and appearances of piety, so that the men whom it beguiles find it difficult to detect its various aspects.

Mark the Ascetic

Give me Your grace, good Lord, to count the world as nothing; to set my mind firmly on You and not to hang on the blasting words of men's mouths.

Thomas More

What men call fame is, after all, but a thing full of wind. A man thinks that many are praising him, and talking only of him, and yet they spend but a very small part of the day thinking of him, being occupied with things of their own.

Thomas More

Christ tells us that if we want to join Him, we will travel the way He took. Surely it is not right that the Son of God should go His way on the path of shame while the sons of men walk the way of worldly honor.

John of Avila

We crush the head of the serpent when we scorn and trample underfoot the glory of the world, the praises, the vanities and all the other pomps of pride.

Marie of the Incarnation

The saints were so completely dead to themselves that they cared very little whether others agreed with them or not.

John Vianney

Those who covet honor, I mean a great name, really covet no substantial thing at all.

John Henry Cardinal Newman

HOPE

Hope always draws the soul from the beauty that is seen to what is beyond, always kindles the desire for the hidden through what is perceived.

Gregory of Nyssa

The most hopeful people in the world are the young and the drunk: the first because they have little experience of failure, and the second because they have succeeded in drowning theirs.

Thomas Aquinas

Hide yourself in Jesus crucified, and hope for nothing except that all men be thoroughly converted to His will.

Paul of the Cross

HUMAN NATURE

For it is impossible for our human nature ever to stop moving; it has been made by its Creator ever to keep changing. Hence when we prevent it from using up its energy on trifles, and keep it on all sides from doing what it should not, it must necessarily move in a straight path towards truth.

Gregory of Nyssa

Men go abroad to wonder at the height of mountains, at the huge waves of the sea, at the long courses of the rivers, at the vast compass of the ocean, at the circular motion of the stars—yet they pass by themselves without wondering.

Augustine of Hippo

Our condition is most noble, being so beloved of the most high God that He was willing to die for our sake—which He would not have done if man had not been a most noble creature and of great worth.

Angela of Foligno

It is not our body that feels, not our mind that thinks, but we, as single human beings, who both feel and think.

Thomas Aquinas

God is like a mother who carries her child in her arms by the edge of a precipice. While she is seeking all the time to keep him from danger, he is doing his best to get into it.

John Vianney

HUMILITY

It is to the humble that Christ belongs, not to those who exalt themselves above His flock. Our Lord Jesus Christ, the Scepter of God's majesty, did not come in the pomp of pride or arrogance—though He could have done so—but rather in humility.

Pope Clement I

I saw all the devil's traps set upon the earth, and I groaned and said, "Who do you think can pass through them?" And I heard a voice saying, "Humility."

Antony the Great

As a ship cannot be built without nails, so a person cannot be saved without humility.

Amma Syncletice

Whoever subjects himself to his neighbor in love can never be humiliated.

Basil the Great

Let us with great diligence implant in our souls the mother of all things that are good—I mean humility.

John Chrysostom

If you should ask me what are the ways of God, I would tell you that the first is humility, the second is humility, and the third is still humility. Not that there are no other precepts to give, but if humility does not precede all that we do, our efforts are fruitless.

Augustine of Hippo

Do you wish to rise? Begin by descending. Do you plan a tower that will pierce the clouds? First lay the foundation on humility.

Augustine of Hippo

Those who stumble on level ground should stay away from cliffs.

Pope Gregory the Great

We descend by self-exaltation and ascend by humility.

Benedict of Nursia

Humility is the only virtue no devil can imitate.

John Climacus

Humility is a divine veil that covers our good deeds and hides them from our own eyes.

John Climacus

Blessed is the one who takes no more pride in the good that God says and does through him than in that which He says and does through someone else.

Francis of Assisi

What a man is before God, that he is, and nothing more.

Francis of Assisi

You should never praise anyone until you see how he turns out in the end.

Francis of Assisi

An artist who paints our Lord or the Blessed Virgin honors them and recalls them to our mind; nevertheless, the painting claims no other merit than what it is, a creation made of wood and color. God's servant is like a painting: a creature of God, through whom God is honored because of His blessings. He must not lay claim to any more merit than the wood and color do.

Francis of Assisi

All this reverence that is paid to me I never take to myself, but I simply pass it all on to God.

Francis of Assisi

Whoever will proudly dispute and contradict will always stand outside the door. Christ, the master of humility, manifests His truth only to the humble and hides Himself from the proud.

Vincent Ferrer

It constantly happens that the Lord permits a soul to fall so that it may grow humbler. When it is honest, and realizes what it has done, and returns, it makes ever-increasing progress in our Lord's service.

Teresa of Avila

[To argue] over who is the more noble is nothing more than to dispute whether dirt is better for making bricks or for making mortar. O my God! What an insignificant matter!

Teresa of Avila

God always gives a greater blessing to humble beginnings than to those that start with a chiming of bells.

Vincent de Paul

What was the life of Christ but a perpetual humiliation?

Vincent de Paul

Humility is to the various virtues what the chain is in a rosary. Take away the chain and the beads are scattered; remove humility, and all virtues vanish.

John Vianney

I knew nothing; I was nothing. For this reason God picked me out.

Catherine Laboure

The gate of heaven is very low; only the humble can enter it.

Elizabeth Ann Seton

On her retirement to a hidden life in the cloister after her celebrated public life as a visionary:
The Blessed Virgin used me like a broom, and then put me back in my place. I'm glad of it, and there I stay.

Bernadette Soubirous

HYPOCRISY

You are like a house with a highly ornamented façade, where burglars have stolen all the furniture out of the back door.

Antony the Great

If a man preaches but does not practice what he preaches, he is like a well of water where everyone can quench his thirst and wash off his dirt, but which cannot clean away the filth and dung that is around it.

Abba Poemen

Whoever denies Christ in his actions is an antichrist. Instead of listening to what he says, I look at the life he leads. When actions speak loudly, who needs words? For what evil man doesn't want to speak well?... The worst liar is the antichrist who with his mouth professes that Jesus is the Christ, but by his actions denies Him.

Augustine of Hippo

Whoever bids other folks to do right, but gives an evil example by acting the opposite way, is like a foolish weaver who weaves quickly with one hand and unravels the cloth just as quickly with the other.

Thomas More

Hypocrisy and true virtue have a great resemblance in their external appearance, but they are easily distinguished from each other. Hypocrisy cannot long continue, but is quickly dissipated like rising smoke, while true virtue is always firm and constant.

Francis de Sales

IDLENESS

The idle child treasures up misery for its gray hairs.

Herve of Brittany

Idleness is the enemy of the soul.

Benedict of Nursia

Always be doing something worthwhile; then the Devil will always find you busy.

Francis of Assisi

The principal trap that the Devil sets for young people is idleness. This is a fatal source of all evil. Don't let there be any doubt in your mind that man is born to work, and when he doesn't do so, he's out of his element and in great danger of offending God.

John Bosco

THE IMAGE OF GOD IN HUMANITY

When he saw that man was made in the image and likeness of God, the Devil realized that it was useless for him to fight against God, so instead he entangled God's image in evil. In the same way, an angry man might throw stones at the emperor's image, since he cannot throw them at the emperor, and so must be content with striking the wood that bears his likeness.

Basil the Great

Try to realize the dignity God has bestowed on you: He created and formed your body in the image of His beloved Son, and your soul in His own likeness. Yet every creature under heaven serves, acknowledges, and obeys its Creator in its own way better than you do.

Francis of Assisi

The dignity of resembling the Almighty is common to all men; we should then love them all as ourselves, as living images of the Deity.

Francis de Sales

IMAGES, SACRED

Even if we make images of pious men, it is not so that we might adore them as gods, but that when we see them, we might be prompted to imitate them; and if we make images of Christ, it is so that our minds might soar aloft in yearning for Him.

Cyril of Alexandria

In former times God, who is without form or body, could never be depicted. But now that God has been seen in the flesh conversing with men, I make an image of the God whom I see. I do not worship matter; I worship the Creator of matter who became matter for my sake, who willed to take His abode in matter; who worked out my salvation through matter.... Because of this I salute all remaining matter with reverence, because God has filled it with His grace and power.

John of Damascus

What the book is to the literate, the image is to the illiterate. Just as words speak to the ear, so the image speaks to the sight; it brings understanding.

John of Damascus

Demons fear the saints and flee from their shadow. A shadow is an image; therefore I make images to terrify the demons.

John of Damascus

The icon is a hymn of triumph, a showing forth, a memorial inscribed for those who have fought and conquered, humbling the demons and putting them to flight.

John of Damascus

THE INCARNATION

Invisible in His own nature, He became visible in ours. Beyond our grasp, He chose to come within our grasp. Existing before time began, He began to exist at a moment in time. Incapable of suffering as God, He did not refuse to be a man, capable of suffering. Immortal, He chose to be subject to the laws of death.

Pope Leo the Great

Neither is there any other cause of the Incarnation except this alone: He saw us bowed down to the ground, perishing, tyrannized by death; and He had mercy.

John Chrysostom

The One who is our very Life descended into our world, and bore our death, and slew it with the abundance of His own life. Thundering, He called out to us to return to Him in heaven.

Augustine of Hippo

Blessed be the Shepherd who became a Lamb for our reconciliation! Blessed be the Branch who became the Cup of our redemption! Blessed also be the Cluster, Fount of the medicine of life! Blessed also be the Tiller, who became Wheat, so that He might be sown; and a Sheaf, so that He might be cut down. Blessed be the Architect who became a Tower for our place of safety!

Ephraem the Syrian

Blessed be He who dwelt in the womb, and wrought within it a perfect Temple so that He might dwell in it, a Throne so that He might be seated in it, a Garment so that He might be arrayed in it, and a Weapon so that He might conquer through it!

Ephraem the Syrian

If the Incarnation was a fantasy, salvation is also a fantasy.

Cyril of Jerusalem

O loving wisdom of our God! When all was sin and shame,
A second Adam to the fight and to the rescue came.
O wisest love! That flesh and blood, which did in Adam fail
Should strive afresh against the foe, should strive and should prevail.
And that a higher gift than grace should flesh and blood refine:
God's presence and His very self and essence all-divine.

John Henry Cardinal Newman

INTELLIGENCE

Let everyone who has the grace of intelligence fear that, because of it, he will be judged more heavily if he is negligent. Let him who has no intelligence or talent rejoice and do as much as he can with the little that he has; for he has been freed from many occasions of sin.

Bridget of Sweden

JESUS — *See also Christ*

When placed on the rack to be tortured for her faith:
Know, tyrant, that you cannot pluck my faith from my heart! Jesus Christ is my all-in-all, He is my treasure, my life, my bliss, my capitol, my temple, my altar, and nothing can separate me from Him!

Macra

Jesus, the very thought of Thee with sweetness fills my breast;
But sweeter far Thy face to see, and in Thy presence rest.

Bernard of Clairvaux

Nothing is mine, I no longer have anything but Jesus. No place, no thing, no person, no thought, no feelings, no honors, no suffering can turn me away from Jesus. He is for me honor, delight, heart and soul. He whom I love is fatherland, Heaven already! My treasure! My love! Jesus, and Jesus crucified alone makes my happiness!

Bernadette Soubirous

Jesus makes the bitterest mouthful taste sweet.

Thérèse of Lisieux

Oh, if everyone were to know how beautiful Jesus is, how amiable He is! They would all die from love.

Gemma Galgani

JESUS, THE NAME OF

For the name of Christ is on the lips of all: It is invoked by the just man in the service of justice; by the perjurer for the sake of deceiving; by the king to confirm his rule; by the soldier to nerve himself for battle; by the husband to establish his authority; by the wife to confess her submission.... All invoke the name of Christ, the Christian with true reverence, the pagan with feigned respect; and they shall all undoubtedly give to that same Person whom they invoke an account both of the spirit and of the language in which they repeat His name.

Augustine of Hippo

No voice can sing, nor heart can frame, nor can the mem'ry find
A sweeter sound than Thy blest name, O Savior of mankind.

Bernard of Clairvaux

Nothing restrains anger, curbs pride, heals the wound of malice, bridles self-indulgence, quenches the passions, checks avarice and puts unclean thoughts to flight as does the name of Jesus.

Bernard of Clairvaux

JOY, DELIGHT — *See also Laughter; Sadness*

When many men rejoice together, there is a richer joy in each individual, since they enkindle themselves and they inflame one another.

Augustine of Hippo

I have not yet thought or said, O Lord, how much Your blessed ones will rejoice. Surely, they will rejoice in the degree that they will love. And they will love in the degree that they will know. How much will they know You in that day, Lord; how much will they love You?

Anselm of Canterbury

For I have found a joy that is full, and more than full. For when heart, and mind, and soul, and all the man, are full of that joy, joy beyond measure will still remain. Therefore, the whole of that joy shall not enter into those who rejoice; rather, they who rejoice shall enter fully into that joy.

Anselm of Canterbury

No misery is more genuine than false joy.

Bernard of Clairvaux

When spiritual joy fills hearts, the Serpent throws off his deadly poison in vain. The devils cannot harm the servant of Christ when they see he is filled with holy joy.

Francis of Assisi

What are God's servants but His minstrels, who must inspire the hearts of men and stir them to spiritual joy!

Francis of Assisi

If the servant of God, as may happen, is disturbed in any way, he should rise immediately to pray, and he should remain in the presence of the heavenly Father until He restores to him the joy of salvation. For if he remain stupefied in sadness … it will generate an abiding rust in the heart.

Francis of Assisi

In God alone is there primordial and true delight, and in all our delights it is this delight that we are seeking.

Bonaventure

The very sight of God causes delight. Hence he who sees God cannot be without delight.

Thomas Aquinas

No man truly has joy unless he lives in love.

Thomas Aquinas

No one can live without delight, and that is why a man deprived of spiritual joy goes over to carnal pleasures.

Thomas Aquinas

From silly devotions and from sour-faced saints, good Lord, deliver us.

Teresa of Avila

A glad spirit attains to perfection more quickly than any other.

Philip Neri

Live in holy joy and fly from anything that would dissipate your spirit.

Paul of the Cross

Be merry, really merry. The life of a true Christian should be a perpetual jubilee, a prelude to the festivals of eternity.

Theophane Venard

JUDGMENT, DIVINE

We must busy ourselves with preparations for our departure from this world. For even if the day when the whole world ends never overtakes us, the end of each of us is right at the door.

John Chrysostom

When we will have come to Judgment Day, we will then recognize the justice of all God's decisions.

Augustine of Hippo

Judgment cannot be pronounced on a man until he has run his course.

Thomas Aquinas

Everyone—past, present and future—will be judged.... Now, then, is the time for mercy, while the time to come will be the time for justice only. For that reason, the present time is ours, but the future time will be God's only.

Thomas Aquinas

There are four remedies against the fear of divine judgment. The first is good deeds.... The second is confession and repentance of the evil done—and this should include three conditions: sorrow of heart, shame in confession, and rigor of satisfaction. These atone for eternal punishment. The third is almsdeeds, which cleanse us from all stains.... The fourth is charity, namely, the love of God and our neighbor.

Thomas Aquinas

The day that is past must not judge the day that is present, nor the present day judge that which is past; it is only the Last Day that judges all.

Francis de Sales

That day of doom, one and the same for the collected world—that solemn consummation for all flesh, is, in the case of each, anticipate upon his death.

John Henry Cardinal Newman

JUSTICE

The rule of justice is plain: namely, that a good man ought not to swerve from the truth, nor inflict any unjust loss on anyone, nor act in any way deceitfully or fraudulently.

Ambrose of Milan

Justice ... is the virtue that gives to each his due.

Augustine of Hippo

Let justice be done though the world perish.

Augustine of Hippo

A society of men is just only if it obeys You.

Augustine of Hippo

Justice is a certain rectitude of mind whereby a man does what he ought to do in the circumstances confronting him.

Thomas Aquinas

Two main reasons why men fall short of justice: deference to magnates, and deference to the mob.

Thomas Aquinas

Act like a seller when you're buying, and a buyer when you're selling, and then you'll sell and buy justly.

Francis de Sales

THE KINGDOM OF GOD

"Thy kingdom come.".... Christ Himself, dearest brothers, is the kingdom of God, whom we day by day desire to come, whose advent we crave to be quickly manifested to us. For since He Himself is the Resurrection, because in Him we rise again, so also the kingdom of God may be understood to be Himself, because in Him we shall reign.

Cyprian of Carthage

KNOWLEDGE —*See also Education, Learning*

There are some points on which ignorance is better than knowledge.

Augustine of Hippo

If knowledge can cause most people to become vain, perhaps ignorance and lack of learning can make them humble. Yet now and then you do find men who pride themselves in their ignorance.

John Climacus

What have you to be proud of? If you were so clever and learned that you knew everything and could speak every language, so that the things of heaven were an open book to you, still you could not boast of that. Any one of the demons once knew more about the things of heaven, and now knows more about the things of earth, than any human being, even one who might have received from God a special revelation of the highest wisdom.

Francis of Assisi

If you desire to know ... ask grace, not instruction; desire, not understanding; the groaning of prayer, not diligent reading; the Spouse, not the teacher; God, not man; darkness, not clarity; not light, but the fire that totally inflames and carries us into God by ecstatic unctions and burning affections.

Bonaventure

The end of my labors has come. All that I have written appears to me as so much straw after the things that have been revealed to me.

Thomas Aquinas

LAUGHTER— *See also Joy, Delight; Sadness*

In order to be worthy of the things of heaven, you must laugh to scorn things present.

John Chrysostom

Give me a sense of humor, Lord, and something to laugh about.

Thomas More

In this short season of sowing in this weeping world, we must water our seed with the showers of our tears—and then we will have in heaven a merry, laughing harvest forever.

Thomas More

Laugh and grow strong.

Ignatius Loyola

Joy, with peace, is the sister of charity.... Serve the Lord with laughter.

Padre Pio of Pietrelcina

LEADERS, LEADERSHIP

He who has undertaken the governing of souls must prepare himself to render to God an account of them.

Benedict of Nursia

Those who are put in charge of others should be no prouder of their office than if they had been appointed to wash the feet of their comrades. They should be no more upset at the loss of their authority than they would be if they were deprived of the task of washing feet. The more they are upset, the greater the risk they incur to their souls.

Francis of Assisi

Be on such simple, cordial terms with those under you that when you are all together, it would be impossible to say which is the superior.

Vincent de Paul

LENT, THE SEASON OF

Have you run so many circles of the years bustling vainly about the world, and yet you don't have forty days to be free for prayer for your own soul's sake?

Cyril of Jerusalem

The glory of these forty days we celebrate with songs of praise;
For Christ, by whom all things were made, Himself has fasted and has prayed.
Alone and fasting Moses saw the loving God who gave the Law;
And to Elijah, fasting, came the steeds and chariots of flame.
So Daniel trained his mystic sight, delivered from the lion's might;
And John, the Bridegroom's friend, became the herald of Messiah's name.
Then grant us, Lord, like them to be full oft in fast and prayer with Thee;
Our spirits strengthen with Thy grace, and give us joy to see Thy face.

Pope Gregory the Great

LISTENING TO GOD

It is true that the voice of God, having once penetrated the heart, becomes strong as the tempest and loud as the thunder. But before reaching the heart it is as weak as a light breath that scarcely agitates the air. It shrinks from noise and is silent amid agitation.

Ignatius Loyola

When it's God who is speaking ... the proper way to behave is to imitate someone who has an irresistible curiosity and who listens at keyholes. You must listen to everything God says at the keyhole of your heart.

John Vianney

THE LITURGY

Try to gather more frequently to celebrate God's Eucharist and to praise Him. For when you meet with frequency, Satan's powers are overthrown and his destructiveness is undone by the unanimity of your faith.

Ignatius of Antioch

The whole sanctuary and the space before the altar is filled with the heavenly Powers come to honor Him who is present upon the altar.

John Chrysostom

Think now of what kind of choir you are about to enter. Although clothed with a body, you have been judged worthy to join the Powers of heaven in singing the praises of Him who is Lord of all!

John Chrysostom

How I wept when I heard Your hymns and canticles, being deeply moved by the sweet singing of Your Church. Those voices flowed into my ears, truth filtered into my heart, and from my heart surged waves of devotion.

Augustine of Hippo

In the dispensation of Christ's mysteries, there is at once the power of grace and the encouragement of teaching, so that He whom we confess in the spirit of faith we may follow in the example of our work.

Pope Leo the Great

Ceremonies may be shadows, but they are the shadows of great truths, and it is essential that they should be carried out with the greatest possible attention.

Vincent de Paul

To me nothing is so consoling, so piercing, so thrilling, so overcoming, as the Mass.... It is not a mere form of words—it is a great action, the greatest action that can be on earth. It is, not the invocation merely, but, if I dare use the word, the evocation of the Eternal.

John Henry Cardinal Newman

LONGING FOR GOD

The whole life of a good Christian is a holy desire to see God as He is. Now what you long for, you do not yet see, but longing makes you capable of being filled when at last you behold what you have desired.... God, by making us wait in hope, stretches our desire; by making us desire, He stretches our soul; by stretching our soul, He makes it capable of holding more. So let us desire, brothers, for we shall be filled.

Augustine of Hippo

Lord our God, grant us grace to desire You with our whole heart, so that desiring, we may seek and find You; and so finding You, we may love You; and loving You, we may hate those sins from which You have redeemed us.

Anselm of Canterbury

Give me, good Lord, a longing to be with You.

Thomas More

LOVE — *See also Charity; Loving God*

If love dwells in you, you have no enemy on earth.

Ephraem the Syrian

He who has the love of Christ sometimes causes pain, even to someone he loves, for that person's good.

Basil the Great

Here is the rule: Love, and do what you will.

Augustine of Hippo

In order to discover the character of a people, we have only to observe what they love.

Augustine of Hippo

Love alone distinguishes between the children of God and the children of the Devil. They may all sign themselves with the sign of the cross of Christ; they may all respond "Amen" to prayers and sing "Alleluia"; they may all be baptized, and come to church, and even build the church themselves. But we can discern the children of God from the children of the Devil by their love alone.

Augustine of Hippo

Those who have love are born of God; those who have no love are not born of God. This is the great sign, the great distinction. Possess whatever you want, but if you are lacking this one thing, the rest will be of no value to you.

Augustine of Hippo

Christ made love the stairway that would enable all Christians to climb to heaven. Hold fast to it, therefore, in all sincerity, give one another practical proof of it, and by your progress, make your ascent together.

Fulgence of Ruspe

What is the mark of love for your neighbor? Not to seek what is for your own benefit, but what is for the benefit of the one loved, both in body and in soul.

Basil the Great

The way of salvation is easy; it is enough to love.

Margaret of Cortona

If our love for something causes us to break God's commandment, then we love it better than we love God—and that is a love both deadly and damnable.

Thomas More

At the end of life, we will be judged by love.

John of the Cross

The soul cannot live without love. All depends on providing it with a worthy object.

Francis de Sales

We cannot help conforming ourselves to what we love.

Francis de Sales

Love ... transforms the lover into the one loved.

Paul of the Cross

You've got to love while you're suffering and suffer while you're loving.

John Vianney

We are born to love, we live to love, and we will die to love still more.

Joseph Cafasso

If the Church was a body composed of different members, it couldn't lack the noblest of all; it must have a heart, and a heart burning with love. And I realized that this love was the true motive force that enabled the other members of the Church to act; if it ceased to function, the Apostles would forget to preach the Gospel, the Martyrs would refuse to shed their blood.

Thérèse of Lisieux

Love ... is the vocation that includes all others.

Thérèse of Lisieux

Love ... is a universe of its own, comprising all time and space.

Thérèse of Lisieux

Love cannot be content without condescending—condescending to mere nothingness, and making this nothingness the fuel for its flame.

Thérèse of Lisieux

Even a little child can scatter flowers, to scent the throne room with their fragrance; even a little child can sing, in its shrill treble, the great canticle of Love. That shall be my life: to scatter flowers—to miss no single opportunity of making some small sacrifice, here by a smiling look, there by a kindly word, always doing the tiniest things right, and doing it for love.

Thérèse of Lisieux

Perfect love means putting up with other people's shortcomings, feeling no surprise at their weaknesses, finding encouragement even in the slightest evidence of good qualities in them.

Thérèse of Lisieux

LOVING GOD

What is the mark of a love for God? To keep His commandments for the sake of His glory.

Basil the Great

The good things that you love are from Him, and to the extent that they are used for Him, they will remain both good and pleasant. But the things that come from Him will be rightly turned into bitterness if they are not rightly loved—if God is forsaken because you have a greater love for what He has created.

Augustine of Hippo

In the long run there will be but two kinds of men: those who love God and those who love something else.

Augustine of Hippo

The reason for loving God is God Himself; the measure of loving God is to love Him beyond measure.

Bernard of Clairvaux

Love Him totally who gave Himself totally for your love.

Clare of Assisi

Give me, good Lord, such a love for You that I will love nothing in a way that displeases You, and I will love everything for Your sake.

Thomas More

Oh, that we might all be mad for love of Him who for love of us was called mad!

Teresa of Avila

Like the bee that sucks honey from all the wildflowers and will not use them for anything else, the soul easily extracts the sweetness of love from all the things that happen to her, that is, she loves God in them. Thus everything leads her to love always the delight of loving God.

John of the Cross

To love God you need three hearts in one: a heart of fire for Him, a heart of flesh for your neighbor, and a heart of bronze for yourself.

Benedict Joseph Labre

It is always springtime in the heart that loves God.

John Vianney

LUST

A lustful horse and an unchaste human body should have their feed reduced.

Hilarion

The stuffing of the stomach is the hotbed of lust.

Jerome

By lust I mean that affection of the mind that aims at the enjoyment of one's self and one's neighbor without reference to God.

Augustine of Hippo

Sinful lust is not nature, but a disease of nature.

Augustine of Hippo

Lust indulged became habit, and habit unresisted became necessity.

Augustine of Hippo

The time is coming [once we are perfected in heaven] when we shall enjoy one another's beauty without any lust.

Augustine of Hippo

Our relentless enemy, the teacher of fornication, whispers that God is lenient and particularly merciful to this passion, since it is so very natural. Yet if we watch the wiles of the demons, we will observe that after we have actually sinned, they will affirm that God is a just and inexorable judge. They say one thing to lead us into sin, another thing to overwhelm us in despair.

John Climacus

Oh, loathe the love whose final aim is lust, moth of the mind, eclipse of reason's light; the grave of grace ... the wrong of every right. In sum, an evil whose harm no tongue can tell, in which to live is death, to die is hell.

Robert Southwell

MAN, MANKIND

The glory of God is man fully alive.

Irenaeus of Lyons

God did not make the first man because He needed company, but because He wanted someone to whom He could show His generosity and love.

Irenaeus of Lyons

MARRIAGE — *See also Family*

There is a certain love deeply seated in our nature that imperceptibly knits together these bodies of ours.... Nothing so welds our life together as the love of man and wife.

John Chrysostom

The first natural tie of human society is man and wife.

Augustine of Hippo

Marriage is a good in which the married are better in proportion as they fear God more chastely and more faithfully, especially if they also nourish spiritually the children whom they desire carnally.

Augustine of Hippo

Perfect married life means the spiritual dedication of the parents for the benefit of their children.

Thomas Aquinas

Marriage has three blessings. The first is children, to be received and raised for God's service. The second is the loyal faithfulness by which each serves the other. The third is the sacrament of matrimony, which signifies the inseparable union of Christ with His Church.

Thomas Aquinas

Even as you seek a virtuous, fair, and good spouse ... it is fitting that you should be the same.

Bernardino of Siena

The state of marriage is one that requires more virtue and constancy than any other. It is a perpetual exercise in mortification.

Frances de Sales

All the wealth of the world cannot be compared with the happiness of living together happily united.

Margaret of Youville

MARTYRS, MARTYRDOM

On the way to his martyrdom:
How glorious to be a setting sun—setting on the world, on my way to God! May I rise in His presence!

Ignatius of Antioch

I am God's wheat, and I am being ground by the teeth of wild beasts to make a pure loaf for Christ.

Ignatius of Antioch

Now is the moment when I begin to be a disciple. May nothing seen or unseen distract me from making my way to Jesus Christ. Fire, cross, struggles with wild beasts, wrenching of bones, mangling of limbs, crushing of the whole body, cruel tortures inflicted by the Devil—let them come, provided that I make my way to Jesus Christ.

Ignatius of Antioch

When given the choice of cursing Christ or being put to death:
Eighty-six years I have served Him, and He never did me any wrong. How can I blaspheme my King and my Savior?

Polycarp of Smyrna

When given the choice between death or apostasy with marriage to a pagan:
I have a Bridegroom in the heavens, eternal, with all celestial glory as His dower.

Febronia

He cannot claim to be a martyr who has not lived in brotherly love.

Cyprian of Carthage

Bless the martyrs heartily, that you may be a martyr by intention. Thus, even though you depart this life without persecutor, fire, or lash, you will still be found worthy of the same reward.

Basil the Great

The ashes of martyrs drive away demons.

John Chrysostom

The martyrs were bound, imprisoned, scourged, racked, burned, torn apart, butchered—and they multiplied.

Augustine of Hippo

The death of the martyrs blossoms in the faith of the living.

Pope Gregory the Great

When about to be martyred:
Come, my sweetest Jesus, that I may now be inseparably united to Thee in time and eternity: Welcome ropes, hurdles, gibbets, knives, and butchery, welcome for the love of Jesus, my Savior.

Henry Morse

To his captors as they led him on his way to martyrdom:
Why should you bind me? From whom should I escape? From God?

Joseph Mukasa Balikuddembe

To his executioners:

A fountain fed from many springs will never dry up. When we are gone, others will rise in our place.

Bruno Serunkuma of Uganda

No one is a martyr for a conclusion; no one is a martyr for an opinion; it is faith that makes martyrs.

John Henry Cardinal Newman

A martyrdom is a season of God's especial power in the eye of faith, as great as if a miracle were visibly wrought.

John Henry Cardinal Newman

MARY, THE BLESSED VIRGIN

He who is devout to the Virgin Mother will certainly never be lost.

Ignatius of Antioch

The knot of Eve's disobedience was loosed by the obedience of Mary. The knot which the virgin Eve tied by her unbelief, the Virgin Mary opened by her belief.

Irenaeus of Lyons

What a wonder is Your mother! The Lord entered her, and became a Servant; the Word entered her, and became silent within her; Thunder entered her, and His voice was still; the Shepherd of all entered her, and He became a Lamb in her, and came forth bleating.... The Rich went in; He came out poor; the Most High went in; He came out lowly. Brightness went into her and clothed Himself and came forth in the form of One despised ... He who gives food to all went in, and got hunger; He who gives all to drink went in and got thirst. From her came forth naked and bare the One who clothes all.

Ephraem the Syrian

Him whom the heavens cannot contain, the womb of one woman bore. She ruled our Ruler; she carried Him in whom we are; she gave milk to our Bread.

Augustine of Hippo

Far be it that anyone should try to defraud holy Mary of her privileges of divine grace and of her special glory. For by a certain singular favor of our Lord and God, and of her Son, she must be confessed to be the most true and most blessed Mother of God.

Vincent of Lerins

A Virgin conceived, a Virgin bore, and a Virgin she remains.

Peter Chrysologus

A gentle maiden, having lodged a God in her womb, asks as its price: peace for the world, salvation for those who are lost, and life for the dead.

Peter Chrysologus

The God whom earth and sea and sky adore and laud and magnify,
Whose might they own, whose praise they tell, in Mary's body deigned to
  dwell.
O Mother blest! And chosen shrine wherein the Architect divine
Whose hand contains the earth and sky vouchsafed in hidden guise to lie;
Blest in the message Gabriel brought; blest in the work the Spirit wrought;
Most blest, to bring to human birth the long desired of all the earth!

Venantius Fortunatus

O blessed and ever-blessed Virgin, by whose blessing not only is every creature blessed by its Creator, but the Creator is blessed by the creature!

Anselm of Canterbury

In dangers, in doubts, in difficulties, think of Mary, call upon Mary. Don't let her name depart from your lips; never allow it to leave your heart. And that you may more surely obtain the assistance of her prayer, don't neglect to walk in her footsteps.

Bernard of Clairvaux

If the hurricanes of temptation rise against you, or you are running upon the rocks of trouble, look to the star—call on Mary!

Bernard of Clairvaux

It was fitting for the Queen of Virgins, by a singular privilege of sanctity, to lead a life entirely free from sin, so that while she ministered to the Destroyer of death and sin, she should obtain the gift of life and justice for all.

Bernard of Clairvaux

I greet you, Lady, Holy Queen, Holy Mary, Mother of God, Virgin who became the Church, chosen by the most holy Father of heaven; consecrated to holiness through His most holy and beloved Son and the Holy Spirit, the Comforter. In you was and is the whole fullness of grace and everything that is good.

Francis of Assisi

No angel, no saint, can equal her in the multitude and accumulation of heavenly good things.

Bonaventure

As sailors are guided by a star to the port, so Christians are guided to heaven by Mary.

Thomas Aquinas

Eve sought the fruit, but did not find there what she wished for. In her fruit the blessed Virgin found all that Eve had wanted.

Thomas Aquinas

The Blessed Virgin, by becoming the mother of God, received a kind of infinite dignity because God is infinite; this dignity therefore is such a reality that a better one is not possible, just as nothing can be better than God.

Thomas Aquinas

There is no sinner in the world, however much at enmity with God, who cannot recover God's grace by recourse to Mary, and by asking her assistance.

Bridget of Sweden

When a fire is kindled and many logs surround it, the log most apt and efficient for combustion will be the quickest to catch the flame and burn. So it was with Mary. For when the fire of divine love—which in itself is changeless and eternal—began to kindle and appear, and when the Godhead willed to become incarnate, no creature was more apt and efficient for receiving this fire of love than the Virgin Mary; for no creature burned with such charity as she.

Bridget of Sweden

Behold the power of the Virgin Mother: She wounded and took captive the heart of God.

Bernardino of Siena

As flies are driven away by a great fire, so were the evil spirits driven away by her ardent love for God.

Bernardino of Siena

Hail, God's palace; hail, tabernacle of the Most High; hail, house of God; hail, His holy vestments; hail, handmaid of God!

Francis of Assisi

Only after the Last Judgment will Mary get any rest; from now until then, she is much too busy with her children.

John Vianney

All our perfection consists in being conformed, united, and consecrated to Jesus Christ; and therefore the most perfect of all devotions is, without any doubt, that which most perfectly conforms, unites, and consecrates us to Jesus Christ. Now, Mary being the most conformed of all creatures to Jesus Christ, it follows that of all devotions, that which most consecrates and conforms the soul to our Lord is devotion to His holy Mother, and that the more a soul is consecrated to Mary, the more it is consecrated to Jesus.

Louis de Montfort

We consecrate ourselves at one and the same time to the most holy Virgin and to Jesus Christ: to the most holy Virgin as to the perfect means that Jesus Christ Himself has chosen by which to unite Himself to us, and us to Him; and to our Lord as to our Last End, to whom as our Redeemer and our God, we owe all we are.

Louis de Montfort

Mary is the heart of the Church. This is why all works of charity spring from her. It is well known that the heart has two movements: systole and diastole. Thus Mary is always performing these two movements: absorbing grace from her Most Holy Son, and pouring it forth on sinners.

Anthony Mary Claret

The weapon of the second Eve and Mother of God is prayer.

John Henry Cardinal Newman

In her, the destinies of the world were to be reversed, and the serpent's head bruised. In her was bestowed the greatest honor ever put upon any individual of our fallen race. God was taking upon Him her flesh, and humbling Himself to be called her offspring—such is the deep mystery!

John Henry Cardinal Newman

Mother dear, lend me your heart. I look for it each day to pour my troubles into.

Gemma Galgani

MARY, THE ASSUMPTION OF

We in our exile have sent on ahead of us our advocate who, as mother of our Judge and mother of mercy, will humbly and effectively look after everything that concerns our salvation. Today earth has sent a priceless gift up to heaven, so that by giving and receiving within the blessed bond of friendship, the human is wedded to the divine, earth to heaven, the depths to the heights.... Blessed indeed is Mary, blessed in many ways, both in receiving the Savior, and in being received by the Savior.

Bernard of Clairvaux

And who, I ask, could believe that the ark of holiness, the dwelling place of the Word of God, the temple of the Holy Spirit, could be reduced to ruin? My soul is filled with horror at the thought that this virginal flesh that had begotten God, had brought Him into the world, had nourished and carried Him, could have been turned into ashes or given over to be the food of worms.

Robert Cardinal Bellarmine

MARY, THE BIRTH OF

Today, the reformation of our nature begins, and the aging world is transformed anew to the divine likeness and receives the beginnings of a second formation by God.

Andrew of Crete

MARY, THE QUEENSHIP OF

Assuredly, she who played the part of the Creator's servant and mother is in all strictness and truth in reality God's mother and lady and queen over all created things.

John of Damascus

To serve Mary and to be her courtier is the greatest honor one can possibly possess, for to serve the Queen of Heaven is already to reign there, and to live under her commands is more than to govern.

John of Damascus

Just as Mary surpassed in grace all others on earth, so also in heaven is her glory unique. If eye has not seen or ear heard or the human heart conceived what God has prepared for those who love Him [1 Cor 2:9], who can express what He has prepared for the woman who gave Him birth and who loved Him, as everyone knows, more than anyone else?

Bernard of Clairvaux

She has surpassed the riches of the virgins, the confessors, the martyrs, the apostles, the prophets, the patriarchs, and the angels, for she herself is the first-fruit of the virgins, the mirror of confessors, the rose of martyrs, the ruler of apostles, the oracle of prophets, the daughter of patriarchs, the queen of angels.

Bonaventure

No one has access to the Almighty as His mother has; none has merit such as hers. Her Son will deny her nothing that she asks; and herein lies her power. While she defends the Church, neither height nor depth, neither men nor evil spirits, neither great monarchs, nor craft of man, nor popular violence, can avail to harm us; for human life is short, but Mary reigns above, a Queen forever.

John Henry Cardinal Newman

MARY MAGDALENE

The Magdalene, most of all, is the model I like to follow. That boldness of hers, which would be so amazing if it weren't the boldness of a lover, won the heart of Jesus, and how it fascinates mine!

Thérèse of Lisieux

THE MASS — *See Liturgy*

MEDITATION, RECOLLECTION

God knows how to bring it about that a man enjoys meditation as if he were going to a dance. Or on the other hand, He knows how to let one experience meditation as if struggling in battle.

Nicholas of Flue

Above all I recommend to you always, recollection, that holy solitude, that inner sacred desert in which your soul ought always to be alone in the bosom of the heavenly Father, in the silence of faith and holy love.

Paul of the Cross

MERCY, DIVINE

God turns Himself away, not so much from those who sin, as from those who aren't stricken with fear after they sin.

John Chrysostom

Our Lord came first as Medicine, not as Judge. For if He had come to judge first, He would have found no one on whom He might bestow the rewards of righteousness. Since, then, He saw that all were sinners, and that no one was exempt from the sentence of death that followed sin, His mercy had to be sought first, before His judgment could be executed.

Augustine of Hippo

No one should feel secure in this life, because the whole of it is one long test; and no one who is able to pass from a worse state to a better one can be certain that he will not later also pass from a better state to a worse. Our only hope, our only confidence, our only assured promise, Lord, is Your mercy.

Augustine of Hippo

God never deserts a man, unless first He is deserted by that man. For even if a man shall have committed grievous sins once, and twice, and a third time, God still looks for him, just as He says through the prophet, "so that he may be converted and live."

Caesarius of Arles

God has promised pardon to the one who repents, but He has not promised repentance to the one who sins.

Anselm of Canterbury

Mercy is the fulfillment of justice, not its abolition.

Thomas Aquinas

If someone, at the Devil's prompting, had committed every sin against God and then, with true contrition and the intention of amendment, truly repented these sins and humbly, with burning love, asked God for mercy, there is no doubt that the kind and merciful God Himself would immediately be as ready to receive that person back into His grace with great joy and happiness as would be a loving father who saw returning to him his only, dearly beloved son, now freed from a great scandal and a most shameful death.

Bridget of Sweden

No mother could snatch her child from a burning building more swiftly than God is constrained to succor a penitent soul.

Henry Suso

Since God displayed His great mercy in so many ways even toward Judas, an apostle turned traitor, since He invited him so often to be forgiven and did not allow him to perish except through despair alone, surely there is no cause for anyone in this life to despair even of an imitator of Judas.

Thomas More

Where is the foolish person who would think it in his power to commit a sin more than God could forgive?

Francis de Sales

Our sins are nothing but a grain of sand alongside the great mountain of the mercy of God.

John Vianney

Had He so pleased, He might have found, when we sinned, other beings to do Him service, casting us into hell; but He purposed to save and to change *us*.

John Henry Cardinal Newman

MIRACLES

Those who crucified our Lord supposed when He was dead that His signs had died with Him. But His signs manifestly continued to live through His disciples, so that the murderers might know that the Lord of the signs was living.

Ephraem the Syrian

If God has given you the power, go ahead and work a miracle; that's why He gave you the power. But don't think that those who have never worked a miracle aren't part of the kingdom of God.

Augustine of Hippo

God is always almighty; He can at all times work miracles, and He would work them now as in the days of old were it not that faith is lacking!

John Vianney

The incarnation is the most stupendous event which ever can take place on earth; and after it and henceforth, I do not see how we can scruple at any miracle on the mere ground of its being unlikely to happen.

John Henry Cardinal Newman

MODERNISM

Undoubtedly, were anyone to attempt the task of collecting together all the errors that have been broached against the faith and to concentrate into one the sap and substance of them all, he could not succeed in doing so better than the Modernists have done. No, they have gone further than this, for ... their system means the destruction not of the Catholic religion alone, but of all religion.

Pope Pius X

MONEY — *See Wealth*

MONKS — *See Religious Life*

MORTIFICATION

The mortified man is able to suck honey from the rock and oil from the rugged stones.

Bernard of Clairvaux

The soul should treat the body as its child, correcting without hurting it.

Francis of Assisi

Certain virtues are greatly esteemed and always preferred by the general run of men because they are close at hand, easily noticed, and in effect material. Thus many people prefer bodily to spiritual alms; hairshirts, fasting, going barefoot, using the discipline, and physical mortifications to meekness, patience, modesty, and other mortifications of the heart, although the latter are really higher virtues.

Francis de Sales

They who pay a moderate attention to the mortification of their bodies and direct their main attention to mortify the will and understanding, even in the matters of the slightest moment, are more to be esteemed than those who give themselves exclusively to bodily penances.

Philip Neri

The perfection of a Christian consists in mortifying himself for the love of Christ. Where there is no great mortification, there is no great sanctity.

Philip Neri

The best way not to find the bed too cold is to go to bed colder than the bed is.

Charles Cardinal Borromeo

The practices of mortification should be modified by prudence and the advice of a wise director, because it often happens that the Devil urges a soul to excessive penances to tire her and render her unfit for the service of God and the fulfillment of her duties.

Anna Maria Taigi

In the convent we are without shoes and stockings; we shall see if we can stand it. It's certain that on the one hand, we don't want to pamper anyone, but on the other hand, we don't want to kill anyone, either.

Mary Magdalen Bentivoglio

MYSTERY

When we say this thing is a mystery, of the *thing* we say nothing, but of ourselves we say that we do not comprehend this thing—as defect of strength in us makes some weights to be immobile, so likewise defect of understanding makes some truths to be mysterious.

Elizabeth Ann Seton

Mysteries in religion are measured by the proud according to their own capacity; by the humble, according to the power of God: the humble glorify God for them, the proud exalt themselves against them.

John Henry Cardinal Newman

A revelation is religious doctrine viewed on its illuminated side; a mystery is the selfsame doctrine viewed on the side unilluminated.

John Henry Cardinal Newman

THE NATIVITY OF CHRIST—*See Christmas*

NECESSITY

You make a virtue of necessity.

Jerome

Necessity has no law.

Augustine of Hippo

NEIGHBORS

When you see your brother, you see God.

Clement of Alexandria

The sign that you love God is this: that you love your fellow. And if you hate your fellow, your hatred is toward God.

Ephraem the Syrian

If you are angry at your neighbor, you are angry at God.... Honor your neighbor, and you have honored God.

Ephraem the Syrian

From our neighbor are life and death. If we do good to our neighbor, we do good to God; if we cause our neighbor to stumble, we sin against Christ.

Anthony the Great

Suppose we were to ... draw the outline of a circle.... Let us suppose that this circle is the world, and that God Himself is the center; the straight lines drawn from the circumference are the lives of men.... The closer those lines are to God, the closer they become to one another; and the closer they are to one another, the closer they become to God.

Dorotheos of Gaza

God said: I have placed you in the midst of your fellows so that you may do to them what you cannot do to Me—that is, so that you may love your neighbor freely without expecting any return from him. And what you do to him I count as done to Me.

Catherine of Siena

It is impossible to fulfill the law concerning love for Me, God eternal, apart from the law concerning love for your neighbors. These are the two feet of affection on which you must follow the commandments and counsels given you by Christ crucified.

Catherine of Siena

We cannot be sure whether we are loving God, although we may have good reasons for believing that we are. But we can know quite well whether we are loving our neighbor.

Teresa of Avila

Though we do not have our Lord with us in bodily presence, we have our neighbor; who, for the ends of love and loving service, is as good as our Lord Himself.

Teresa of Avila

Don't think that, because the particular virtues you have in mind don't shine in your neighbor, he won't be precious in God's sight for something you're not thinking about.

John of the Cross

We can never love our neighbor too much.

Francis de Sales

NOVELISTS
Novelists are generally great liars.

Jean Baptiste de la Salle

NOVELTY
Far, far from the clergy be the love of novelty! God hates the proud and the obstinate mind.

Pope Pius X

NUNS — *See Religious Life; Virgins, Consecrated*

OBEDIENCE TO GOD
God did not tell us to follow Him because He needed our help, but because He knew that loving Him would make us whole.

Irenaeus of Lyons

Whoever doesn't have one Master has many.

Ambrose of Milan

Attempts to be virtuous that are joined to disobedience to the will of God, no matter how good they may appear, will actually work for our damnation.

Thomas More

No man may legitimately do what God has forbidden nor leave undone what God has commanded by claiming that he does so according to his own private understanding of what reverence or devotion requires. For this would be an imprudent devotion, and an irreverent reverence, and not at all a proper humility. It is instead only an unrecognized pride to stand stubbornly against God's will and to disobey His pleasure.

Thomas More

God desires the least degree of obedience and submissiveness more than all those services you think of rendering Him.

John of the Cross

Don't think that pleasing God lies so much in doing a great deal as in doing it with good will, without possessiveness and the approval of men.

John of the Cross

What does it profit you to give God one thing if He asks of you another? Consider what it is God wants, and then do it.

John of the Cross

The mind [must be] ever on the alert to discover the indications of Providence, and the will prepared to carry them out.

Vincent de Paul

You must refuse nothing you recognize to be His will.

Jane Frances de Chantal

OBEDIENCE TO RELIGIOUS SUPERIORS

Obedience is the only virtue that implants the other virtues in the heart and preserves them after they have been so implanted.

Pope Gregory the Great

Obedience is the sepulcher of the will and the resurrection of lowliness.

John Climacus

Obedience is the perfection of the religious life; by it man submits to man for the love of God, as God rendered Himself obedient unto men for their salvation.

Thomas Aquinas

The Devil doesn't fear austerity but holy obedience.

Francis de Sales

Obedience is a little dog that leads the blind.

Joseph of Cupertino

OBSTINACY

If a man begins to continue in his sins, despair is born of the multitude of those sins, and obstinacy is begotten of despair.... God does not compel anyone to be obstinate; obstinacy results rather from His indulgence and forgiveness. Thus it must be believed that it was not divine power but divine patience that hardened Pharaoh.

Caesarius of Arles

OPPORTUNITY

He who loses an opportunity is like the man who lets a bird fly from his hand, for he will never recover it.

John of the Cross

THE OUR FATHER

What can be a more spiritual prayer than the one that was given to us by Christ, who also gave us the Holy Spirit? What prayer to the Father can be more truthful than the one that was delivered to us by the Son who is Truth, from His own mouth?... Let us therefore, beloved brothers, pray as God our Teacher has taught us. It is a loving and friendly prayer to beseech God with His own word, to approach His ears in the prayer of Christ. Let the Father acknowledge the words of His Son when we make our prayer, and let the One who dwells within our breast Himself also dwell in our voice. And since we have Him as an Advocate with the Father for our sins, when as sinners we petition on behalf of our sins, let us put forward the words of our Advocate.

Cyprian of Carthage

We don't say "My Father, who art in heaven," nor "Give me this day my daily bread"; nor does each one ask that only his own debt should be forgiven him; nor does he request for himself alone that he may not be led into temptation and may be delivered from evil. Our prayer is public and common; and when we pray, we pray not for one, but for the whole people, because we the whole people are one.

Cyprian of Carthage

What mysteries are contained in the Our Father! How many and how great are they, collected briefly in words, but spiritually abundant in virtue! There is absolutely nothing passed over that is not comprehended in these our prayers and petitions—a summary of heavenly doctrine!

Cyprian of Carthage

It ought to excite us to praise God exceedingly when we consider the great excellence of this heavenly prayer, composed as it was so well by such a good Master, so that, daughters, every one of us may apply it to our needs. I am astonished to see how every kind of contemplation and perfection is comprised in such few words; for if we study only this book, we seem to stand in need of no other. Herein our Lord has already taught us every kind of prayer.

Teresa of Avila

THE OUR FATHER AND HAIL MARY

At each word of the Our Father, Hail Mary, and Glory Be, I glimpse an abyss of goodness and mercy.

Anthony Mary Claret

Sometimes, when I'm in such a state of spiritual dryness that I can't find a single thought in my mind that will bring me close to God, I say an Our Father and a Hail Mary very slowly indeed. How they take me out of myself then!

Thérèse of Lisieux

THE PASSIONS

A movement of the soul contrary to nature in the sense of disobedience to reason: that is what passions are.

Clement of Alexandria

For each of our impulses, when it takes control, becomes the master and we the slave. Like a tyrant it seizes the citadel of the soul, and by means of its underlings plays havoc with its subjects, using our own thoughts as the servants of its good pleasure.

Gregory of Nyssa

Anger, fear, cowardice, arrogance, pleasure, grief, hatred, spite, heartless cruelty, jealousy, flattery, bearing grudges and resentment, and all the other hostile drives within us: There is your array of the masters and tyrants that try to enslave the soul, their prisoner of war, and bring it under their control.

Gregory of Nyssa

A man who governs his passions is master of the world. We must either command them, or be commanded by them. It is better to be a hammer than an anvil.

Dominic

PATIENCE

Patient endurance is the perfection of charity.

Ambrose of Milan

Patience is the companion of wisdom.

Augustine of Hippo

Patience is the root and guardian of all the virtues.

Pope Gregory the Great

Let your understanding strengthen your patience. In serenity look forward to the joy that follows sadness.

Peter Damian

We can never know how patient or humble someone is when everything is going well with him. But when those who should cooperate with him do exactly the opposite, then we can know. A man has as much patience and humility as he has then, and no more.

Francis of Assisi

He submitted Himself to the elements, to cold and heat, hunger and thirst ... concealing His power and giving it up, taking on the likeness of man, so that He might teach us weak and wretched mortals with what patience we ought to bear tribulation.

Angela of Foligno

Patient endurance attains to all things. The one who possesses God is lacking in nothing; God alone is enough.

Teresa of Avila

When you encounter difficulties and contradictions, don't try to break them, but bend them with gentleness and time.

Francis de Sales

Have patience with all the world, but first of all with yourself.

Francis de Sales

When you are excited to impatience, think for a moment how much more reason God has to be angry with you, than you can have for anger against any human being; and yet how constant is His patience and forbearance.

Elizabeth Anne Seton

PEACE

Peace ... is the tranquillity of order.

Augustine of Hippo

Belligerents are not reluctant to have peace, but they want a peace to their own liking.

Augustine of Hippo

Peace is always in God, for God is peace and peace cannot be destroyed, but discord is destroyed.

Nicholas of Flue

Lord, make me an instrument of your peace; where there is hatred, let me sow love; where there is injury, pardon; where there is doubt, faith; where there is despair, hope; where there is darkness, light; and where there is sadness, joy. O Divine Master, grant that I may not so much seek to be consoled as to console; to be understood as to understand; to be loved as to love; for it is in giving that we receive, it is in pardoning that we are pardoned, and it is in dying that we are born to eternal life.

Francis of Assisi

Peace is better than a fortune.

Francis de Sales

The Christian has a deep, silent, hidden peace, which the world sees not, like some well in a retired and shady place.

John Henry Cardinal Newman

PENANCE — *See Confession, Penance*

PENTECOST

The Church and the world have need of a new Pentecost, a second Pentecost, a priestly Pentecost, an interior Pentecost.

Concepcion Cabrera de Armida

PERFECTION

By the perfect exercise of only one virtue, a man may attain to the height of all the rest.

Gregory Nazianzen

No one is suddenly made perfect.

Bede the Venerable

Perfection does not consist in consolation, but rather in the submission of our wills to God—above all, in desolation.

Henry Suso

Our perfection certainly consists in knowing God and ourselves.

Angela of Foligno

Perfection: Is it not a loving, sweet union of the will with that of God?

Vincent de Paul

There are certain souls who desire to arrive at perfection all at once, and this desire keeps them constantly unsettled. It is necessary first to cling to the feet of Jesus, then to kiss His sacred hands, and at last you may find your way into His divine heart.

Alphonsus Liguori

We can never attain to perfection while we have an affection for any imperfection.

Francis de Sales

Don't wish to be anything but what you are, and try to be that perfectly.

Francis de Sales

We must not be disturbed at our imperfections, since for us perfection consists in fighting against them. How can we fight against them unless we see them, or overcome them unless we face them?

Francis de Sales

Don't worry about your perfection, or about your soul. God to whom it belongs, and to whom you have completely entrusted it, will take care of it and fill it with all the graces, consolations and blessings of His holy love in the measure that they will be useful in this life.

Jane Frances de Chantal

Walk in the good, believe in God, don't try to acquire perfection by force, but do everything quietly and then you will be truly humble. God will give you everything.

Paul of the Cross

The highest perfection is to nourish yourself on the divine will in a spirit of pure faith and love.

Paul of the Cross

Christian perfection consists in three things: praying heroically, working heroically, and suffering heroically.

Anthony Mary Claret

PERSECUTION

Be devoted to God and do not fear, for no wounds can come to those who follow Christ. Even if they take away the life of your body, Christ is still with you.

Ambrose of Milan

It is frequently in pain of the body, amid the very hands of persecutors, that Christ is really found.... In a little while, in a brief moment, when you have escaped the hands of your persecutors, and have not given in to the ways of the world, Christ will meet you and will not allow you to be tempted further.

Ambrose of Milan

Nothing is more to be feared than too long a peace. You are deceived if you think that a Christian can live without persecution. He suffers the greatest persecution of all who lives under none. A storm puts a man on his guard and obliges him to exert his utmost efforts to avoid shipwreck.

Jerome

The instance cannot be found in the history of mankind, in which an anti-Christian power could long abstain from persecution.

John Henry Cardinal Newman

PERSEVERANCE

The woman who stayed behind [at the tomb] to seek Christ was the only one who saw Him. For perseverance is essential to any good deed, as the Voice of truth tells us: "Whoever perseveres to the end will be saved" [Mt 10:22].

Pope Gregory the Great

We ought to make some progress, however little, every day, and show some increase of fervor. We ought to act as if we were at war—as, indeed, we are—and never relax until we have won the victory.

Teresa of Avila

Let me get through today, and I shall not fear tomorrow.

Philip Neri

My Jesus, if You uphold me, I shall not fall.

Philip Neri

Though perseverance does not come from our power, yet it comes within our power.

Francis de Sales

The little daily lesson: to keep soberly and quietly in His Presence, trying to turn every little action on His Will; and to praise and love through cloud and sunshine is all my care and study.

Elizabeth Ann Seton

PETER, SAINT

O foundation of the Church blessed in calling him by this new name, O rock worthy to be built upon, which will dissolve the laws of hell, the gates of Tartarus, and all the bonds of death! O blessed doorkeeper of heaven, to whose judgment the keys of access to eternity are committed, whose earthly sentence is binding authority in heaven.

Hilary of Poitiers

It is to Peter himself that He says: "You are Peter, and upon this rock I will build My Church" [Mt 16:18]. Where Peter is, there is the Church. And where the Church is, no death is there, but eternal life.

Ambrose of Milan

Peter, the leader of the choir, the mouth of all the apostles, the head of that tribe, the ruler of the whole world, the foundation of the Church, the ardent lover of Christ.

John Chrysostom

PLAY

A saint was once asked, while playing happily with his companions, what he would do if an angel told him that in a quarter of an hour he would die and have to appear before the judgment seat of God. The saint promptly replied that he would continue playing because he was certain these games were pleasing to God.

John Bosco

POETRY, POETS

Poetry is the wine of devils.

Augustine of Hippo

Poets and philosophers are alike in being big with wonder.

Thomas Aquinas

The Church herself is the most sacred and august of poets.

John Henry Cardinal Newman

POLITICS

Nations don't rise to supremacy through merit; their fortunes vary at random.

Cyprian of Carthage

When did a royal alliance ever begin in good faith or end without bloodshed?

Cyprian of Carthage

To the Roman imperial prefect about to execute him for his faith:
The glory we look forward to is spiritual, heavenly, not of this world, for this world passes away, and all the glory of it. But what is laid up for us in the heavens is eternal, which God has prepared for those who believe in Him. And what are you and your princes, but smoke that is blown away by the storm?

Venantius of Camerino

Rulers are custodians of the decrees of God.

Basil the Great

It is right to submit to higher authority whenever a command of God would not be violated.

Basil the Great

The difference between good and bad emperors is that the good love freedom; the bad, slavery.

Ambrose of Milan

Rulers are happy if they rule justly.

Augustine of Hippo

If justice is taken away, then, what are kingdoms but great robberies?

Augustine of Hippo

Paraphrasing the Roman orator Cicero:
A first-rate power will not engage in war except either for honor or for safety.

Augustine of Hippo

God overthrows the thrones of those who are disobedient to His law.

Avitus of Vienna

Sanctify yourself, and you will sanctify society.

Francis of Assisi

Let the holy one pray, and the prudent one rule.

Thomas Aquinas

The government of tyrants cannot last long because it is hateful to the multitude, and what is against the wishes of the multitude cannot long be preserved.

Thomas Aquinas

The Christian is bound to obey the authorities when their power is from God, but not otherwise.

Thomas Aquinas

Human government is derived from the divine government and should imitate it.

Thomas Aquinas

The purpose of temporal tranquillity, which well-ordered policies establish and maintain, is to give opportunities for contemplating truth.

Thomas Aquinas

The world would have peace if only the men of politics would follow the Gospels.

Bridget of Sweden

My political views are those of the Our Father.

John Bosco

If He turns their poisonous joys into bitterness, if He corrupts their pleasures, and if He scatters thorns along the path of their riot, paths hitherto strewn with the roses of laughter, the reason is that He loves them still. And this is the holy cruelty of the Physician, who, in extreme cases of sickness, makes us take most bitter and most horrible medicines.... The greatest mercy of God is not to let those nations remain in peace with each other who are not at peace with God.

Padre Pio of Pietrelcina

THE POOR

When you have pity on the poor, you lend to God; and whoever gives to the least, gives to God—a sweet-smelling spiritual sacrifice to Him.

Cyprian of Carthage

After selling his copy of the Gospels and giving the money to those who were hungry:
I have sold the book that told me to sell all that I had and give to the poor.

Serapion

The bread you store up belongs to the hungry; the cloak that lies in your chest belongs to the naked; the gold that you have hidden in the ground belongs to the poor.

Basil the Great

Let us relieve the poverty of those who beg from us; and if they impose upon us, let us not be over-exact about it.

John Chrysostom

Love knows that among the poor, and especially among the blind, there are people who shine like the sun, cleansed by their endurance and the ills they have suffered.

Simeon the Insane

Whoever curses a poor man does an injury to Christ, whose noble image he wears—the image of Him who made Himself poor for us in this world.

Francis of Assisi

Even though the poor are often rough and unrefined, we must not judge them from external appearances nor from the mental gifts they seem to have received. On the contrary, if you consider the poor in the light of faith, then you will observe that they are taking the place of the Son of God who chose to be poor.

Vincent de Paul

THE POPE, THE PAPACY

By pointing out the tradition which that very great, oldest, and well-known Church—founded and established at Rome by those two most glorious apostles, Peter and Paul—received from the apostles, I can put to shame all of those who in any way, either through wicked self-conceit, or through vainglory, or through blind and evil opinion, gather together in a way they should not. For every Church must be in harmony with this Church because of its outstanding pre-eminence, that is, the faithful from every-where, since the apostolic tradition is preserved in it by those from every-where.

Irenaeus of Lyons

It is on Peter that He builds the Church, and to him that He entrusts the sheep to feed. And although He assigns a like power to all the Apostles, yet He founded a single chair, thus establishing by His own authority the source and hallmark of the Church's unity.

Cyprian of Carthage

If a man does not hold fast to this unity of Peter, does he imagine that he still holds the faith? If he deserts the chair of Peter upon whom the Church was built, does he still have confidence that he is in the Church?

Cyprian of Carthage

To Pope Damasus:
I follow no leader but Christ and join in communion with none but Your Blessedness, that is, with the chair of Peter. I know that this is the rock on which the Church has been built. Whoever eats the Lamb outside this house is profane. Anyone who is not in the ark of Noah will perish when the flood prevails.

Jerome

Reckon up the priests from the days that Peter sat, and in their ancestral ranks note who succeeded whom; for that is the Rock over which the gates of hell shall never prevail.

Augustine of Hippo

Rome has spoken; the matter is settled.

Augustine of Hippo

The Roman Church has never erred and, according to Scripture, never shall err.

Pope Gregory VII

Only the Church of Peter, to whose lot fell Italy when the disciples were sent out to preach, has always stood fast in the faith. While the faith has disappeared or has partly decayed in other regions, the Church of Peter still flourishes in faith and free from heresy.

Thomas Aquinas

To Pope Gregory XI:
Take care that I do not have to complain about you to Jesus crucified. There is no one else I can complain to, for you have no superior on earth.

Catherine of Siena

POVERTY

He is rich enough who is poor in Christ.

Jerome

A man's poverty before God is judged by the disposition of his heart, not by his coffers.

Augustine of Hippo

Poverty was not found in heaven. It abounded on earth, but man did not know its value. The Son of God, therefore, treasured it and came down from heaven to choose it for Himself, to make it precious to us.

Bernard of Clairvaux

No man should commend poverty unless he is poor.

Bernard of Clairvaux

Poverty I love, but not dirt.

Bernard of Clairvaux

If we had any possessions, we would be forced to have arms to protect them, since possessions are a cause of disputes and strife, and in many ways we would be hindered from loving God and our neighbor. Therefore in this life we wish to have no temporal possessions.

Francis of Assisi

Poverty is the special way of salvation. It is the source of humility and the root of all perfection, and its fruit is manifold, though unseen. This is the treasure hidden in the field in the Gospel, to buy which we must sell all—and anything that cannot be sold should be abandoned for love of it.

Francis of Assisi

To desire to be poor but not to be inconvenienced by poverty, is to desire the honor of poverty and the convenience of riches.

Francis de Sales

Alas! I have nothing to bequeath to you but my bad example.

Paul of the Cross

POVERTY OF SPIRIT

Try to practice real poverty of spirit. Live completely detached from every consolation of sense, both within and without, to prevent falling into the trap of spiritual gluttony. It is necessary to live detached from your own pleasure, from your own way of thinking and feeling, so as not to fall prey to spiritual dilettantism.

Paul of the Cross

To the poor in spirit the kingdom of heaven is assigned as a present recompense, for theirs *is* the kingdom of heaven. This is so because to those who are truly poor in spirit, the Lord gives great helps, even in this life.

Alphonsus Liguori

THE PRAISE OF GOD

All our life is like a day of celebration for us; we are convinced, in fact, that God is always everywhere. We work while singing; we sail while reciting hymns; we accomplish all other occupations of life while praying.

Clement of Alexandria

Blessed be He whom our mouth cannot adequately praise, because His Gift is too great for the skill of orators to tell; neither can human abilities adequately praise His goodness. For, praise Him as we may, it is too little. Yet since it is useless to be silent and constrain ourselves, may our feebleness excuse such praise as we can sing.

Ephraem the Syrian

Ocean of glory who has no need for Your glory to be sung, in your goodness receive this drop of praise, since by Your Gift You have supplied my tongue with the power to glorify You!

Ephraem the Syrian

Happy is the one who becomes a fountain of voices—all of them praising You in all things!

Ephraem the Syrian

Our meditation in this present life should be in the praise of God; for the eternal exultation of our life hereafter will be the praise of God; and none can become fit for the future life who has not practiced himself for it now.

Augustine of Hippo

Say alleluia always, no matter the time of day, no matter the season of life.

Benedict of Nursia

The whole world is asleep, and God, so full of goodness, so great, so worthy of all praise, no one is thinking of Him! See, nature praises Him, and man ... who ought to praise Him, sleeps! Let us go and wake up the universe ... and sing His praises!

Mariam Baouardy

PRAYER

Prayer is conversation with God.

Clement of Alexandria

The Christian prays in every situation, in his walks for recreation, in his dealings with others, in silence, in reading, in all rational pursuits.

Clement of Alexandria

If He who was without sin prayed, how much more ought sinners to pray!

Cyprian of Carthage

Do nothing at all unless you begin with prayer.

Ephraem the Syrian

It is lawful to pray for what it is lawful to desire.

Augustine of Hippo

Learn to pray to God in such a way that you are trusting Him as your Physician to do what He knows is best. Confess to Him the disease, and let Him choose the remedy. Then hold tight to love, for what He does will cut and sting you.

Augustine of Hippo

If you want to "pray without ceasing" [1 Th 5:17], never cease to long for God. The continuation of your longing is the continuation of your prayer; and if you cease to long for Him, this prayer will also cease.

Augustine of Hippo

When we are linked by the power of prayer, we, as it were, hold each other's hand as we walk side by side along a slippery path; and thus by the bounteous disposition of charity, it comes about that the harder each one leans on the other, the more firmly we are riveted together in brotherly love.

Pope Gregory the Great

He causes his prayers to be of more avail to himself, who offers them also for others.

Pope Gregory the Great

Prayer is a wine that makes glad the heart of men.

Bernard of Clairvaux

I would rather say five words devoutly with my heart than five thousand that my soul does not relish with affection and understanding.

Edmund of Abingdon

Day by day, day by day, O dear Lord, three things I pray:
To see Thee more clearly, love Thee more dearly, follow Thee more nearly,
Day by day.

Richard of Chichester

When we pray, the voice of the heart must be heard more than the proceedings from the mouth.

Bonaventure

He prays best who does not know that he is praying.

Anthony of Padua

It is not necessary for us to set forth our petitions before God in order to make known to Him our needs and desires, but rather that we ourselves may realize that in these things it is necessary to have recourse to God's assistance.

Thomas Aquinas

It is an old custom of the saints of God to have some little prayers ready and to be frequently darting them up to heaven during the day, lifting their minds to God out of the mire of this world. He who adopts this plan will obtain great fruits with little pains.

Philip Neri

Vocal prayer ... must be accompanied by reflection. A prayer in which a person is not aware of whom he is speaking to, what he is asking, who it is who is asking and of whom, I don't call prayer—however much the lips may move.

Teresa of Avila

You pay God a compliment by asking great things of Him.

Teresa of Avila

Anyone who has the habit of speaking before God's majesty as if he were speaking to a slave, careless about how he is speaking, and saying whatever comes into his head and whatever he's learned from saying prayers at other times, in my opinion is not praying. Please, God, may no Christian pray in this way.

Teresa of Avila

I would never want any prayer that would not make the virtues grow within me.

Teresa of Avila

Let him never cease from prayer who has once begun it, be his life ever so wicked; for prayer is the way to amend it, and without prayer such amendment will be much more difficult.

Teresa of Avila

The soul at prayer is a rock, because God holds it fast in His infinite love.

Paul of the Cross

Remain in the presence of God; awaken your soul with ejaculatory prayers and with darts of love of God. Rest in His bosom, like a child on its mother's breast, with full and deep confidence.

Paul of the Cross

Aspire to God with short but frequent outpourings of the heart; admire His bounty; invoke His aid; cast yourself in spirit at the foot of His cross; adore His goodness; treat with Him of your salvation; give Him your whole soul a thousand times in the day.

Francis de Sales

Follow your own way of speaking to our Lord sincerely, lovingly, confidently, and simply, as your heart dictates.

Jane Frances de Chantal

The great method of prayer is to have none. If in going to prayer you can form in yourself the pure capacity for receiving the Spirit of God, that will suffice for all method.

Jane Frances de Chantal

As a rule, people are very happy to be able to speak to a king. Those who find it hard to speak to God for half an hour have no discernment!

Vincent de Paul

The air we breathe, the bread we eat, the heart that throbs in our breast, are not more necessary for a man that he may live as a human being, than is prayer for the Christian that he may live as a Christian.

John Eudes

Whoever doesn't give up prayer can't possibly continue to offend God.

Alphonsus Liguori

To approach God, one should go straight to Him, like a ball from a cannon.

John Vianney

The more you pray, the more you want to pray.... It's like a fish that starts by swimming near the surface of the water, then plunges and goes on swimming deeper and deeper. The soul plunges, is swallowed up, loses itself in the delights of conversation with God.

John Vianney

We must pray literally without ceasing—without ceasing; in every occurrence and employment of our lives. You know I mean that prayer of the heart which is independent of place or situation, or which is, rather, a habit of lifting up the heart to God, as in a constant communication with Him.

Elizabeth Ann Seton

How pitiful it is to put our devotion in a multitude of prayers too often repeated, without attention to what we say, and scarcely thinking to whom we are speaking ... without listening to God, who would receive so much more glory from even the shortest adorations proceeding from the heart.

Elizabeth Ann Seton

Remember that God prefers the poverty of our hearts to the most sublime thoughts borrowed from others.

Peter Julian Eymard

We must pray without tiring, for the salvation of mankind does not depend upon material success ... but on Jesus alone.

Frances Xavier Cabrini

Thou art coming to a King; large petitions with thee bring;
For His grace and power are such, none can ever ask too much.

John Henry Cardinal Newman

What an extraordinary thing it is, the efficiency of prayer! Like a queen, it
has access at all times to the royal Presence, and can get whatever it asks for.

Thérèse of Lisieux

I tell God what I want quite simply, without any splendid turns of phrase,
and somehow He always manages to understand me.

Thérèse of Lisieux

Prayer means a launching out of the heart towards God; it means lifting up
one's eyes, quite simply, to heaven, a cry of grateful love, from the crest of
joy or the trough of despair; it's a vast, supernatural force that opens out
my heart and binds me close to Jesus.

Thérèse of Lisieux

It is true that God's power triumphs over everything, but humble and suffering prayer prevails over God Himself.

Padre Pio of Pietrelcina

What is the prayer of the Church, if not the self-giving of the great lovers
to the God who is Love?

Edith Stein

You go to pray: to become a bonfire, a living flame, giving heat and light.

Josemaria Escriva

PRAYER, INATTENTION DURING

At the time of prayer, let the heart be closed against the adversary and open
to God alone, nor let it allow God's enemy to approach it. For frequently
he steals upon us, and penetrates within, and by crafty deceit calls away our
prayers from God, so that we may have one thing in our heart and another
in our voice—at the very time when not the voice, but the soul and mind
should be praying to the Lord with a simple intention. But what carelessness it is to be distracted and carried away by foolish and profane thoughts
when you are praying to the Lord, as if there were anything that you
should rather be thinking of than to think of talking to God!

Cyprian of Carthage

How can you ask to be heard by God when you yourself aren't even paying attention to what you say? How can you want God to remember you when you pray if you yourself don't even remember what you say?

Cyprian of Carthage

If someone, simply as an experiment, should try with determination to make his mind touch on as many and as diverse objects as possible, I hardly think that in so short a time he could run through such diverse and numerous topics as the mind, unrestrained, wanders through while the mouth negligently mutters through the most common prayers.

Thomas More

Our minds do not go wandering while we address an earthly prince about some important matter or even while we speak to one of his ministers who might hold a position of some influence with his master. So surely it could never happen that our minds should stray even a little while we pray to God—surely not, that is, if we believed with a strong, lively faith that we are truly in the presence of God.

Thomas More

What I only aim at is this: that we see Him, and remain with Him, to whom we are speaking, without turning our backs on Him. For I think that is what we do when we keep talking to God while thinking about a thousand trifles at the same time.

Teresa of Avila

PRAYER, POSTURE IN

Let us consider that we are standing in God's sight. We must please the divine eyes with the posture of our body as well as the measure of our voice.

Cyprian of Carthage

A reverent attitude of the body, though it takes its origin and character from the soul, increases by a kind of reflex the soul's own reverence and devotion to God.

Thomas More

Whatever our bodies may be doing, we should at the same time continually lift up our minds to God, which is the most acceptable form of prayer. For no matter which way we may turn our steps, as long as our minds are turned to God, we clearly are not turned away from Him who is present everywhere.

Thomas More

I would insist that, besides the prayers we may say through the day while walking, we also should occasionally say some prayers for which we have prepared our minds more thoughtfully, for which we have disposed our bodies more reverently, than we would if we were about to approach all the rulers in the whole world seated together in one place.

Thomas More

PRAYER, UNANSWERED

We must understand, then, that even though God doesn't always give us what we want, He gives us what we need for our salvation.

Augustine of Hippo

So blind are we in this mortal life, and so unaware of what will happen—so uncertain even of how we will think tomorrow—that God could not take vengeance on a man more easily in this world than by granting his own foolish wishes.

Thomas More

PRAYER AND ACTION

Those who pray should not come to God with fruitless or naked prayers. Petition is ineffective when it is a barren entreaty that beseeches God.... For He who will give us in the day of judgment a reward for our labors and alms is even in this life a merciful hearer of the one who comes to him in prayer associated with good works.

Cyprian of Carthage

Those prayers ascend quickly to God which the merits of our labors urge upon God.

Cyprian of Carthage

Practice should be sustained by prayer, and prayer by practice.

Pope Gregory the Great

The things, good Lord, that I pray for, give me the grace to labor for.

Thomas More

How often I failed in my duty to God, because I was not leaning on the strong pillar of prayer.

Teresa of Avila

Don't imagine that, if you had a great deal of time, you would spend more of it in prayer. Get rid of that idea; it is no hindrance to prayer to spend your time well.

Teresa of Avila

Jacob did not cease to be a saint because he had to attend to his flocks.

Teresa of Avila

The most potent and acceptable prayer is the prayer that leaves the best effects. I don't mean it must immediately fill the soul with desire…. The best effects [are] those that are followed up by actions—when the soul not only desires the honor of God, but really strives for it.

Teresa of Avila

Jacob's ladder … is a faithful representation of the devout life. The two sides between which we ascend, and which support the steps, are prayer, which bring the love of God, and the Sacraments that confer it. The steps are but the various degrees of charity by which we advance from virtue to virtue, either descending in action to the aid of our neighbor, or ascending in contemplation to a loving union with God.

Francis de Sales

Yes, prayer—and preparation, too.

Elizabeth Ann Seton

PRAYER VIGILS

Since in the kingdom we shall possess only day, without the intervention of night, let us watch in the night as if in the daylight. Since we are to pray and give thanks to God forever, let us not cease in this life also to pray and give thanks.

Cyprian of Carthage

Whoever is … wakeful and prayerful in the night, in this visible darkness he is surrounded by an invisible light.

Ephraem the Syrian

The quiet and solitude of the night make it a favorable time for prayer and most suitable for those who watch. With worldly occupations put aside and the attention undivided, the whole man, at night, stands in the divine presence.

Niceta of Remesiana

If we give ourselves to meditation and prayer in the dark silence of the night, the soul, collected, will discover that it is much more open to divine consolation than it is during the daytime, when the noise of business all around distracts the eyes, the ears, and the mind, and dissipates our energy in countless activities that are as meaningless as they are varied.

Thomas More

How is it that even though thoughts about some trivial, worldly matter may at times wake us and keep us awake for a long time, hardly letting us go back to sleep at all, on the other hand prayer somehow fails to keep us awake!

Thomas More

If we try to escape sadness by seeking our consolation in sleep, we will fail to find what we are seeking, for we will lose in sleep the consolation we might have received from God if we had stayed awake and prayed.

Thomas More

PRAYERLESSNESS

Souls who don't practice prayer are like people with paralyzed or crippled bodies; even though they have hands and feet, they can't give orders to their hands and feet.

Teresa of Avila

The man who doesn't pray is like a chicken or a turkey, which can't rise into the air. They may fly a little, but they soon have to come down, they scratch the earth and get deeper and deeper in it, they cover their heads with it and they don't seem to take pleasure in anything else. The man who prays, on the other hand, is like a fearless eagle, and seems always to want to get closer to the Sun.

John Vianney

PREACHERS, PREACHING

Just as God's creature, the sun, is one and the same the world over, so also does the Church's preaching shine everywhere to enlighten all men who want to come to the knowledge of truth.

Irenaeus of Lyons

My own talents are small. But I still have the duty of investing the divine word in the minds of the people. I fear the day when I shall be asked to show the interest accruing.

Ambrose of Milan

The Lord gives a man grace of speech in proportion to the sincerity with which his audience wishes to hear him.

Moses the Black

Human devices for enhancing style should not be employed in preaching the Gospel, lest they conceal the grace of God.

Basil the Great

Those who, to please their listeners, avoid giving a forthright declaration of the will of God become the slaves of those they would please and abandon the service of God.

Basil the Great

Be sure that you first preach by the way you live. If you do not, people will notice that you say one thing, but live otherwise, and your words will bring only cynical laughter and a derisive shake of the head.

Charles Cardinal Borromeo

A preacher is like a trumpet that produces no tone unless one blows into it. Before preaching, pray to God, "You are the Spirit and I am only the trumpet, and without your breath I can give no sound."

Joseph of Cupertino

I must preach so that the most illiterate laborer can understand me.

Alphonsus Liguori

If a parish priest doesn't want to be damned, and if there is any loose living in his parish, he must spurn the very thought of public opinion and the fear of being despised or hated by his parishioners. Even if he were certain of being lynched when he came down from the pulpit, that must not stop him from speaking out against it.

John Vianney

The most powerful orator is not the one who is applauded, but the one who moves all to follow him. When a man is moved to repentance, he thinks only of amending his life, and does not stop to praise anyone.

Dominic Barberi

If the people leave the church praising the preacher, one can be certain that he did not do his duty well. Sighs, not praise, are the proof of effective oratory.

Dominic Barberi

He who speaks to the inhabitants of the stars has no effect on the inhabitants of earth.

Dominic Barberi

Flowers are good, but of no use to the starving.

Dominic Barberi

The true style of oratory, and the most difficult to achieve, is that which seems simple and easy, and leaves the listener with the impression that he could have done just as well himself. The efficacy of preaching lies in plain, natural instruction about the duties of everyman.

Dominic Barberi

When I see the need for divine teaching and how hungry people are to hear it, I am atremble to be off and running throughout the world, preaching the word of God. I have no rest, my soul finds no other relief, than to rush about and preach.

Anthony Mary Claret

PRESUMPTION

Two criminals were crucified with Christ. One was saved; do not despair. One was not; do not presume.

Augustine of Hippo

"God told me," "God replied to me," they assert—and yet most of the time they are talking to themselves.

John of the Cross

Reflect that "many are called but few are chosen" [Mt 22:14], and that—if you're not careful—your damnation is more certain than your salvation, especially since the path to eternal life is so narrow.

John of the Cross

PRIDE, THE PROUD

Don't condemn silver just because you possess gold.

Cyril of Jerusalem

What better proof of your pride could you have given than to claim you were not proud?

John Climacus

Men can heal the lustful. Angels can heal the malicious. Only God can heal the proud.

John Climacus

I think there are few men—though they dare not be so bold to admit it—who don't imagine that if they had been God's advisor in the creation of the world, they could have made it better.

Thomas More

God was so displeased with pride that He did not spare to drive down into hell the noble, high, excellent angels of heaven for the sake of their pride. So who in this wretched world could have a status so high that he would not have serious cause to tremble and quake in every joint of his body as soon as he feels a high, proud thought enter his heart?

Thomas More

Just as men may call the one a fool who bears himself proudly because he struts about in a borrowed suit, so may all of us too be rightly called true fools if we take pride in anything that we have in this life. For nothing we have here is our own, not even our bodies. All that we ever have, we have received from God: riches, royalty, power, beauty, strength, learning, intellect, body, soul, and all.

Thomas More

PRIESTS AND DEACONS

Deacons ... must avoid all reproach as they would beware of fire.

Ignatius of Antioch

The priesthood requires a great soul; for the priest has many harassing troubles of his own, and has need of innumerable eyes on all sides.

John Chrysostom

O venerable dignity of priests, in whose hands the Son of God becomes incarnate anew as He formerly became incarnate in the womb of Mary!

Augustine of Hippo

The government of souls is the art of arts.

Pope Gregory the Great

God said: They are My anointed ones, and I call them My Christs, because I have given them the office of administering Me to you, and have placed them like fragrant flowers in the mystical body of holy Church. The angel himself has no such dignity, for I have given it to those men whom I have chosen for my ministers, and whom I have appointed as earthly angels in this life.

Catherine of Siena

When people want to destroy religion, they start by attacking priests, because where there are no priests, there is no sacrifice; and where there is no sacrifice, there is no religion.

John Vianney

Leave a parish twenty years without a priest, and they'll be worshiping the animals.

John Vianney

Priesthood is the love of the heart of Jesus. When you see a priest, think of our Lord Jesus Christ.

John Vianney

PROVISION, DIVINE

To those who seek God's kingdom and righteousness, He promises that all things shall be added. For since God possesses all things, those who possess God will lack nothing if they do not lack God Himself.

Cyprian of Carthage

God feeds the birds, and daily food is provided to the sparrows; and to creatures that have no sense of divine things, there is no lack of drink or food. Do you think that to a Christian—to a servant of the Lord—to someone given to good works—to someone who is dear to the Lord— anything will be lacking? Do you imagine that the one who feeds Christ is not himself fed by Christ, or that earthly things will be lacking to those to whom heavenly and divine things are given?

Cyprian of Carthage

THE PSALMS

It seems to me that these words of the Psalms become like a mirror to the person singing them, so that he might see himself and the emotions of his soul.

Athanasius of Alexandria

The collection of psalms found in Scripture, composed as it was under the divine inspiration, has from the very beginnings of the Church shown a wonderful power to foster devotion among Christians.

Pope Pius X

PUNISHMENT

It is not right to spare a wrongdoer at the risk of his falling into graver sin.... We must not only do harm to no man, but also restrain him from sin or punish his sin, so that either the man himself who is punished may profit by his experience, or others be warned by his example.

Augustine of Hippo

PURGATORY

Someone says: "It is nothing to me how long I stay in purgatory, so long as I go on finally to eternal life." Let no one say that, beloved brethren, because that purgatorial fire itself will be more difficult than any punishments that can be seen or imagined or felt in this life.

Caesarius of Arles

The greatest suffering of the souls in purgatory ... is their awareness that something in them displeases God, that they have deliberately gone against His great goodness.

Catherine of Genoa

In purgatory ... when God sees the soul pure as it was in its origins, He tugs at it with a glance, and binds it to Himself with a fiery love that by itself could annihilate the immortal soul. In doing so, God so transforms the soul in Him that it knows nothing other than God; and He continues to draw it up into His fiery love until He restores it to that pure state from which it first issued. As it is being drawn upward, the soul feels itself melting in the fire of that love of its sweet God.

Catherine of Genoa

I don't believe it would be possible to find any joy comparable to that of a soul in purgatory, except the joy of the blessed in paradise. For it is a joy that goes on increasing day by day as God more and more flows in upon the soul, which He does abundantly in proportion as every hindrance to His entrance is consumed away.

Catherine of Genoa

Help, Lord, the souls that Thou hast made, the souls to Thee so dear,
In prison for the debt unpaid of sin committed here.
These holy souls, they suffer on, resigned in heart and will,
Until Thy high behest is done, and justice has its fill.
For daily falls, for pardoned crime, they joy to undergo
The shadow of Thy Cross sublime, the remnant of Thy woe.
Oh, by their patience of delay, their hope amid their pain,
Their sacred zeal to burn away disfigurement and stain;
Oh, by their fire of love, not less in keenness than the flame;
Oh, by their very helplessness, Oh, by Thine own great name,
Good Jesus, help! Sweet Jesus, aid the souls to Thee most dear
In prison for the debt unpaid of sins committed here.

John Henry Cardinal Newman

PURITY

Those whose hearts are pure are the temples of the Holy Spirit.

Lucy

Nothing is sweeter than the calm of conscience, nothing safer than purity of soul—yet no one can bestow this on himself because it is properly the gift of Another.

Columbanus

He who aspires to the grace of God must be pure, with a heart as innocent as a child's. Purity of heart is to God like a perfume, sweet and agreeable.

Nicholas of Flue

God desires the least degree of purity of conscience in you more than all the works you can perform.

John of the Cross

The impure then cannot love God; and those who are without love of God cannot really be pure. Purity prepares the soul for love, and love confirms the soul in purity.

John Henry Cardinal Newman

Holy purity, the queen of virtues, the angelic virtue, is a jewel so precious that those who possess it become like the angels of God in heaven, even though clothed in mortal flesh.

John Bosco

QUIET

Quiet is the first step to sanctification.

Basil the Great

READING, SPIRITUAL

You will not see anyone who is truly striving after his spiritual advancement who is not given to spiritual reading.

Athanasius of Alexandria

Listen gladly to holy reading.

Benedict of Nursia

Read some chapter of a devout book…. It is very easy and most necessary, for just as … you speak to God when at prayer, God speaks to you when you read.

Vincent de Paul

REASON, HUMAN

Poor human reason, when it trusts in itself, substitutes the strangest absurdities for the highest divine concepts.

John Chrysostom

Reason is the vision of the mind by means of which it beholds the true.

Augustine of Hippo

God created man to be straightforward, but he has entangled himself with an infinity of questions.

John of Damascus

What is more against reason than to attempt, using reason, to transcend reason itself? And what is more against faith than to be unwilling to believe what reason cannot attain?

Bernard of Clairvaux

Whoever would grasp what he must believe must use reason. Yet reason must not resist faith, but rather walk with her, waiting on her as a handmaid. And even though at times reason seems contrary to faith, yet in truth faith never gets along without her.... Therefore, let your powers of reason be well trained.

Thomas More

Now in the study of Scripture ... I don't deny that the most important thing is to have grace and God's special help. But at the same time, He uses man's reason as an instrument as well. God also helps us to eat—but not without our mouth!

Thomas More

Blessed is he who, setting aside his own liking and inclination, considers things according to reason and righteousness before doing them.

John of the Cross

Reflect that your guardian angel doesn't always prompt your desire for an action, but he does always enlighten your reason. For that reason, in order to practice virtue, don't always wait until you feel like it, for your reason and intellect are sufficient.

John of the Cross

Reason and human science often lead you into error because they are too weak and limited to penetrate to the knowledge of the things of God, which are infinite and incomprehensible. Human intelligence and knowledge also deceive you, because they are too full of darkness and obscurity of sin to attain to a genuine knowledge even of things outside of God.

John Eudes

Right reason, that is, reason rightly exercised, leads the mind to the Catholic faith, and plants it there, and teaches it in all its religious speculations to act under its guidance.

John Henry Cardinal Newman

Reason is one thing, and faith is another, and reason can as little be made a substitute for faith, as faith can be made a substitute for reason.

John Henry Cardinal Newman

Reason can but ascertain the profound difficulties of our condition, it cannot remove them.

John Henry Cardinal Newman

Life is not long enough for a religion of inferences.

John Henry Cardinal Newman

REINCARNATION

I fear lest some absurd reasoning arise to propose that the soul has lived elsewhere, and is afterwards bound to this present body; and that it is from that other life that some receive the gift of prophecy, and that some are condemned, having lived wickedly.... But this is all too absurd, and belongs in no way to the teachings of the Church.

Gregory Nazianzen

RELIGIOUS LIFE— *See also Obedience to Religious Superiors*
Come and see the tents of the soldiers of Christ; come and see their order of battle; they fight every day, and every day defeat and immolate the passions that assail us.

John Chrysostom

The life of a monk ought at all times to be Lenten in its character.

Benedict of Nursia

The poor monk is lord of the world. He has handed over all his cares to God and by his faith has obtained all men as his servants.

John Climacus

He is a monk who has separated his soul from the material world in order to attach himself firmly to God by means of self-control, charity, the singing of psalms, and prayer.

Maximus the Confessor

If there should ever be a monastery without a troublesome and bad-tempered member, it would be necessary to find one and pay him his weight in gold because of the great profit that results from this trial, when good use is made of it.

Bernard of Clairvaux

Each one should confidently make known his need to the other, so that he might find what he needs and minister to him. And each one should love and care for his brother in all those things in which God will give him grace, as a mother loves and cares for her son.

Francis of Assisi

Religious orders are not formed for the purpose of gathering together perfect people, but those who have the courage to aim at perfection.

Francis de Sales

The religious life is not a natural life; it is above nature, and its soul is given and formed by grace.

Francis de Sales

A monastery is an academy of strict correction, where each one should allow himself to be treated, planed, and polished, so that, all the angles being effaced, he may be joined, united, and fastened to the will of God.

Francis de Sales

Poverty should be the badge of the religious; and as men of the world distinguish their property by stamping it with their names, so the works of the religious should be known to be such by the mark of holy poverty.

Mary Magdalene dei Pazzi

REPENTANCE — *See also Confession, Penance*

To the one who still remains in this world, no repentance is too late.

Cyprian of Carthage

The mere renunciation of sins is not sufficient for the salvation of penitents, but fruits worthy of repentance are also required of them.

Basil the Great

Just as men's joy for the world's sake has a sorrow that accompanies it, so also godly tears are a seed of perpetual and unending joy.

John Chrysostom

Properly speaking, there are especially two kinds of compunction: for the soul that thirsts for God is first sorry in his heart from fear, and then from love.

Pope Gregory the Great

Repentance is the returning from the unnatural to the natural state, from the Devil to God, through discipline and effort.

John of Damascus

Good virtuous folks feel more pleasure in the sorrow over their sins and the affliction of their penance than wretches feel in the fulfilling of their foul pleasure.

Thomas More

I wealthiest am when richest in remorse.

Robert Southwell

Where sin was hatched, let tears now wash the nest.

Robert Southwell

I'm certain of this—that if my conscience were burdened with all the sins it's possible to commit, I would still go and throw myself into our Lord's arms, my heart all broken up with contrition; I know what tenderness He has for any prodigal son of His who comes back to Him.

Thérèse of Lisieux

REST

You have made us for Yourself, and our hearts are restless until they find their rest in You.

Augustine of Hippo

I desire rest, but I don't spurn toil. Your will be done.

Martin of Tours

Withdraw often into the depths of your being, and there with living faith rest on the breast of God, like a child, in the sacred silence of faith and holy love.

Paul of the Cross

First tell the Devil to rest, and then I'll rest, too.

John Bosco

Courage! I too must learn to force myself. Even if I am tired, even if exhausted, at the end I can find rest on the heart of Jesus.

Bernadette Soubirous

THE RESURRECTION

In this world sow seeds of righteousness, and in the Resurrection gather them in.

Ephraem the Syrian

God will repair what has been shattered, but not by mending it with something else. Rather, out of the old and very same material of its origin, He will impart to it an appearance of beauty pleasing to Himself.

Hilary of Poitiers

The root of all good works is the hope of the resurrection; for the expectation of the reward is what moves the soul to good works.

Cyril of Jerusalem

Treat this body with care, I pray you, and understand that with this body you will rise from the dead to be judged. But if any thought of doubt should creep into your mind, as though this were impossible, judge what you have not seen by what you have seen. Tell me: Think where you were, you, yourself, a hundred or more years ago.... Can't He, who brought what didn't exist into existence, raise up again what, already in existence, has decayed? Will He, who raises up the grain for us when it dies, year after year, have difficulty in raising us up—those for whose sake the grain has been raised?

Cyril of Jerusalem

If a man is righteous, he will receive a heavenly body, so that he may be able to converse worthily with the angels. But if a man is sinful, he will receive an eternal body fitted to endure the penalties of sin, so that he may burn in the eternal fire without ever being consumed. And justly will God assign to those of either group their portion; for we do nothing without the body. We blaspheme with the mouth; with the mouth we pray. We fornicate with the body; with the body we are chaste. We rob with the hand; with the hand we bestow alms; and the rest in like manner. Since in all things the body has been our agent, it too shall in the future share in the fruits of what has been done.

Cyril of Jerusalem

Just as seed, existing formlessly in the beginning, is shaped into a design and increases in bulk, prepared as it is by the indescribable skill of God, so too it is not at all absurd but entirely consistent that the material enclosed in tombs and which was once possessed of shape should be restored anew to its ancient structure, and dust become man again in the same way that man originally took his birth from dust.

Gregory of Nyssa

The bodies of the saints will therefore rise again free from every defect, from every deformity, and from every corruption, encumbrance, or hindrance. In this way their freedom of action will be as complete as their happiness.

Augustine of Hippo

When we rise again with glorified bodies, in the power of the Lord, these bodies will be white and resplendent as the snow, more brilliant than the sun, more transparent than crystal, and each one will have a special mark of honor and glory, according to the support and endurance of torments and sufferings, willingly and freely borne to the honor of God.

Jan Van Ruysbroeck

REVELATION, DIVINE

Knowing all things, then, and providing for what is profitable for each one, He revealed that which it was to our profit to know; but what we were unable to bear, He kept secret.

John of Damascus

Human salvation demands the divine disclosure of truths surpassing reason.

Thomas Aquinas

As prayer is the voice of man to God, so revelation is the voice of God to man.

John Henry Cardinal Newman

REWARDS, DIVINE

The reward for our more important works is based on our prudent management of lesser ones.

Basil the Great

We lose everything that we leave behind us in this world; we can bring with us only the right to a reward for our charity and the alms we have given. For these we shall receive a reward, a just retribution from God.

Francis of Assisi

His Majesty [the Lord] … rewards great services with trials, and there can be no better reward, for out of trials springs love for God.

Teresa of Avila

That is how His Majesty [the Lord] rewards our good works—I mean, by predisposing us to perform better ones.

Teresa of Avila

May I not come before You with empty hands, since we are rewarded according to our deeds.

Teresa of Avila

I confess that I am bewildered and lose myself at the thought of the divine goodness.... God calls me to an eternal rest after such short and tiny labors ... calls me to heaven, to that Supreme Good that I sought so negligently, and promises me fruit of those tears that I sowed so sparingly.

Aloysius Gonzaga

You are children of eternity. Your immortal crown awaits you, to reward your duty and love. You may indeed sow here in tears, but you may be sure there to reap in joy.

Elizabeth Ann Seton

Nothing seems tiresome or painful when you are working for a Master who pays well; who rewards even a cup of cold water given for love of Him.

Dominic Savio

RIGHTEOUSNESS

Have you begun to stop trying to defend your sins? Then you have made a beginning of righteousness.

Augustine of Hippo

One righteous soul can obtain pardon for a thousand sinners.

Margaret Mary Alacoque

SACRAMENTALS

Where the sign of the cross occurs, magic loses its power, and sorcery has no effect.

Antony the Great

With the sign of the living cross, seal all your doings, my son. Don't go out the door of your house till you have signed the cross. Whether in eating or in drinking, whether in sleeping or in waking, whether in your house or on the road, or again in leisure hours, don't neglect this sign—for there is no guardian like it. It will be for you like a wall in the forefront of all you do.

Ephraem the Syrian

Seal the cross openly on your forehead, so that the demons, seeing the royal sign, will tremble and flee away.

Cyril of Jerusalem

Keep some holy water with you, for there is nothing that puts an evil spirit to flight so effectively.

Teresa of Avila

To decorate their houses with religious pictures is a custom as old as Christianity itself, for the true Christian has always considered his home as nothing less than a temple of God, and the religious pictures as means to extend and preserve the spirit of Christianity in the home.

John Vianney

Let the crucifix be not only in my eyes and on my breast, but in my heart.

Bernadette Soubirous

THE SACRAMENTS — *See also under specific Sacraments*

The gift is bestowed through what is a tangible thing ... but what is accomplished is perceived by the mind.... If you were incorporeal, God would have given you these incorporeal gifts naked. But since the soul is intertwined with the body, He hands over to you in tangible things that which you must perceive by your mind.

John Chrysostom

The spiritual virtue of a sacrament is like light: Although it passes among the impure, it is not polluted.

Augustine of Hippo

What is there awkward about visible and bodily things ministering to spiritual health? Aren't they the instruments of God, who was made flesh for us and suffered in this world?

Thomas Aquinas

Christ's good is communicated to all Christians, even as the power in the head is shared by all the members. This communication is effected by the sacraments of the Church, in which the power of Christ's passion operates, the effect of which is the bestowal of grace for the remission of sins.

Thomas Aquinas

Remember that the purpose of the sacraments is to help us on our way to our last end.

Thomas Aquinas

SACRIFICE

Let us offer Christ the great, universal sacrifice of our love. For He offered His cross to God as sacrifice in order to make us all rich.

Ephraem the Syrian

We should not attach much value to what we have given God, since we shall receive for the little we have bestowed upon Him much more in this life and in the next.

Teresa of Avila

When we must do something we dislike, let us say to God: "My God, I offer You this in honor of the moment when You died for me."

John Vianney

It's a form of trade, you see. I ask God for souls, and pay Him by giving up everything else.

John Bosco

Good is never done except at the expense of those who do it: truth is never enforced except at the sacrifice of its propounders.

John Henry Cardinal Newman

I began to understand that the love of the Sacred Heart without a spirit of sacrifice is but empty illusion.

Maria Droste zu Vischering

The food of real love is sacrifice.

Thérèse of Lisieux

SADNESS

The monks have no sadness. They wage war on the Devil as though they were performing a dance.

John Chrysostom

Let the brothers ever avoid appearing gloomy, sad, and clouded, like the hypocrites; but let us ever be found joyful in the Lord, gay, amiable, gracious, as is fitting.

Francis of Assisi

Melancholy is the poison of devotion. When one is in tribulation, it is necessary to be more happy and more joyful because one is nearer to God.

Clare of Assisi

I will have no sadness in my house.

Philip Neri

A sad saint is a sorry saint.

Francis de Sales

On no account give way to sadness, the enemy of devotion.

Francis de Sales

The evil one is pleased with sadness and melancholy, because he himself is sad and will be so for eternity. Therefore, he desires that everyone should be like himself.

Francis de Sales

Leave sadness to those in the world. We who work for God should be lighthearted.

Leonard of Port Maurice

A hundred years of melancholy and brooding don't pay off a penny of debt.

Dominic Barberi

I want no long-faced saints.

John Bosco

THE SAINTS — *See also Communion of Saints*
Follow the saints, because those who follow them will become saints.

Pope Clement I

We depict Christ as our King and Lord, and we do not strip Him of His army. For the saints are the Lord's army.

John of Damascus

The saints have no need of honor from us; neither does our devotion add the slightest thing to what is theirs. Clearly, if we venerate their memory, it serves us, not them. But I tell you, when I think of them, I feel myself inflamed by tremendous yearning.

Bernard of Clairvaux

The inimitable things in the saints often do us the most good.

Teresa of Avila

Those from whom I receive the greatest consolations and encouragement are those whom I know to be dwelling in Paradise.

Teresa of Avila

SANCTIFICATION, SANCTITY, HOLINESS

The whole science of the saints consists in knowing and following the will of God.

Isidore of Seville

Make me a good man, or let me die young.

Herve of Brittany

Sanctify yourself, and you will sanctify society.

Francis of Assisi

Never do anything that you cannot do in the presence of all.

Teresa of Avila

Sanctity does not consist in being odd, but it does consist in being rare.

Francis de Sales

If you embrace all things in life as coming from the hands of God, and even embrace death to fulfill His holy will, assuredly you will die a saint.

Alphonsus Liguori

Blessed are they who ardently crave sanctity, for their desire shall be fulfilled.

Vincent Pallotti

I greatly desire to become a saint that I may be able to make saints and thus procure the glory of God.

Peter Julian Eymard

Make up your mind to become a saint.

Mary Mazzarello

By holiness we mean the absence of whatever sullies, dims and degrades a rational nature; all that is most opposite and contrary to sin and guilt.

John Henry Cardinal Newman

You cannot be half a saint. You must be a whole saint or no saint at all.

Thérèse of Lisieux

This daring ambition of aspiring to great sanctity has never left me. I don't rely on my own merits, because I haven't any; I put all my confidence in Him who is virtue, who is Holiness itself.

Thérèse of Lisieux

SCANDAL

We should even go beyond doing what is required in order to avoid scandal.

Basil the Great

With regard to doing the will of the Lord, even if someone should be scandalized by what we do, we must not let that hamper our freedom of action.

Basil the Great

SCHISM, SCHISMATICS

Why is it that you harbor strife, bad temper, dissension, schism, and quarreling? Don't we have one God, one Christ, one Spirit of grace that was poured out on us? And isn't there one calling in Christ? Why do we rend and tear apart Christ's members and raise a revolt against our own body?

Pope Clement I

Make no mistake about it. If anyone is not inside the sanctuary, he lacks God's bread.

Ignatius of Antioch

Where there is schism and anger, there is no place for God.

Ignatius of Antioch

Make no mistake, my brothers: If anyone joins himself to a schismatic, he will not inherit God's kingdom. If anyone chooses to be a dissenter, he is cut off from Christ's passion.

Ignatius of Antioch

Be careful, then, to take part in one Eucharist. For there is one flesh of our Lord, Jesus Christ, and one cup of His blood that makes us one, and one altar.

Ignatius of Antioch

Shun schism as the beginning of evil.

Ignatius of Antioch

Separate a ray of the sun from its source of light, and its unity will not allow such a division of light. Break a branch from a tree; when broken, it will not be able to bud. Cut off the stream from its spring, and the stream will dry up. Thus also with the Church.

Cyprian of Carthage

The spouse of Christ cannot be defiled.... Whoever separates from the Church and is joined to an adulteress is separated from the promises of the Church. Nor can he who forsakes the Church of Christ attain to the rewards of Christ: He is a stranger; he is a worldling; he is an enemy.

Cyprian of Carthage

How can the fierceness of wolves dwell in the Christian breast? How the savageness of dogs and the deadly venom of snakes and the bloody cruelty of wild beasts? It is to our benefit when such as these break away from the Church; it keeps them from preying upon the doves and sheep of Christ with their savage, poisonous disease.

Cyprian of Carthage

Let no one think that good men can leave the Church. The wind doesn't carry away the wheat, nor does the hurricane blow down the tree that is firmly rooted. It's the chaff that's swept away by the tempest, and the weakling trees that are uprooted by the blast of the whirlwind.

Cyprian of Carthage

Do they actually think that Christ is with them in their gatherings, when they gather outside the Church of Christ?

Cyprian of Carthage

SCRIPTURES, THE SACRED

But for the searching and right understanding of the Scriptures there is need of a good life and a pure soul, and for Christian virtue to guide the mind to grasp, so far as human nature can, the truth concerning God the Word.

Athanasius of Alexandria

Read the words of Holy Scripture by means of deeds.

Mark the Ascetic

If you would heed the Word of life, cut yourself off from evil things. The hearing of the Word profits nothing to the one who is busy with sins.

Ephraem the Syrian

The study of the inspired Scripture is the chief way of finding our duty.

Basil the Great

Every word and deed should be ratified by the testimony of the Holy Scripture, to confirm those who do good and to shame those who do evil.

Basil the Great

Just as at sea, those who are carried away from the direction of the harbor bring themselves back on course by a clear sign, so Scripture may guide those adrift on the sea of life back into the harbor of the divine will.

Gregory of Nyssa

There is a mirror, a spiritual one ... that not only shows us our own deformity, but transforms it too—if we are willing—into surpassing beauty. This mirror is the memory of good men, and the history of their blessed lives; the reading of the Scriptures; the laws given by God.

John Chrysostom

We ought not, as soon as we leave church, to plunge into business unsuited to church, but as soon as we get home, we should take the Scriptures into our hands, and call our wife and children to join us in putting together what we have heard.

John Chrysostom

Anyone who has received a few coins puts them in a purse and seals it. But we, having been given oracles more precious than gold or costly stones, and receiving the treasures of the Spirit, fail to put them away in the store-houses of our soul! Instead, we thoughtlessly allow them to escape at random from our minds. Who then will pity us, plotting against our own interests, plunging ourselves into so deep a poverty?

John Chrysostom

Divine Scripture is the feast of wisdom, and the individual books are the various dishes.

Ambrose of Milan

Ignorance of the Scriptures is ignorance of Christ.

Jerome

Let sleep find you holding your Bible, and when your head nods, let it be resting on a sacred page.

Jerome

The one who is well grounded in the testimonies of the Scripture is the bulwark of the Church.

Jerome

Let Your Scriptures be my chaste delight. Don't let me be deceived by them or deceive others using them.

Augustine of Hippo

A letter from our fatherland.

Augustine of Hippo

Study your heart in the light of the Holy Scriptures, and you will know therein who you were, who you are, and who you ought to be.

Fulgence of Ruspe

Holy Scripture by the manner of its language transcends every science, because in one and the same sentence, while it describes a fact, it reveals a mystery.

Pope Gregory the Great

The Scripture is a stream in which the elephant may swim and the lamb may wade.

Pope Gregory the Great

Store up in your minds the Lord's words that you receive through your ears, for the Word of the Lord is the nourishment of the mind. When His Word is heard but not stored away in the memory, it is like food that has been eaten and then rejected by an upset stomach. A man's life is despaired of if he cannot retain his food; in the same way, if you receive the food of holy exhortations, but fail to store in your memory those words of life that nurture righteousness, you have good reason to fear the danger of everlasting death.

Pope Gregory the Great

It is good to read the testimonies of Scripture; it is good to seek the Lord our God in them. As for me, however, I have already made so much of Scripture my own that I have more than enough to meditate on and turn over in my mind. I need no more ... I know Christ, the poor crucified One.

Francis of Assisi

Saint Paul tells us, "The letter kills, but the spirit gives life" [2 Cor 3:6]. A man has been killed by the letter of the Sacred Scripture when he wants to quote it only so that people will think him to be very learned,... when he has no desire to follow the spirit of Sacred Scripture, but wants to know what it says only so he can explain it to others.

Francis of Assisi

It is one of the glories of the Scripture that it can embrace many meanings in a single passage.

Thomas Aquinas

Each man marvels to find in the divine Scriptures truths that he himself has thought out.

Thomas Aquinas

By the secret counsel of the Holy Spirit, the Scriptures have been crafted in such a way that they are plain and simple enough for every man to find in them what he needs to understand. Yet again, they are so lofty and difficult that no man is so cunning that he won't find there things far beyond his reach, things far too deep to fathom.

Thomas More

God's word is so rich that it is a treasury of every good. From it flow faith, hope, love, and all the virtues, the many gifts of the Spirit.

Lawrence of Brindisi

God's Word is light to the mind and fire to the will so that a person may know and love the Lord. To the interior person who lives by the Spirit, it is bread and water, but a bread sweeter than any honey from the comb, and water more delicious than milk or wine.

Lawrence of Brindisi

THE SCRIPTURES AND FAITH

Learn to fix the eye of faith on the divine word of the Holy Scriptures as on "a light shining in a dark place until the day dawns and the day-star arises in our hearts" [2 Pet 1:19]. For the ineffable Source from which this lamp borrows its light is the Light that "shines in darkness, but the darkness does not comprehend it" [Jn 1:5]. To see it, our hearts must be purified by faith.

Augustine of Hippo

No matter how lowly a man may be, if he will seek his way through the Scripture with the staff of faith in his hand; and hold that staff, and search out his way with it; and have the holy, ancient teachers of the Church for his guides as well; making his way with good intentions and a lowly heart; using reason and refusing no good learning; calling on God for wisdom, grace, and help that he may keep his way and follow his good guides; then he will never fall into danger, but will wade through surely and well. And he will come to the end of his journey at the place for which he was searching.

Thomas More

THE SCRIPTURES AND THE CATHOLIC CHURCH

If a man will not take the teachings of the Catholic faith as a rule of interpretation when he studies the Scripture—but instead, being distrustful, studies the Scripture to find out whether or not the faith of the Church is true—he cannot fail to fall into errors.

Thomas More

The Church of Christ has always, and never fails in, the right understanding of Scripture, so far as is necessary for our salvation.

Thomas More

If a man should doubt the knowledge and understanding of anything written in the Scripture, he is not wise then to take upon himself the authority to interpret, boldly depending on his own mind. Instead, he should depend on the interpretation of the holy teachers and the saints of old, and on the interpretation that has been received and allowed by the universal Church. For it was the Church through which the Scripture has come into our hands and been delivered to us in the first place, and without the Church, as Saint Augustine says, we could not know which books were Holy Scripture.

Thomas More

From whom did you receive the Sacred Books? From the Church. Which? The Catholic. Then before you can be certain of the authenticity and truthfulness of Sacred Scripture, you must first know which is the true Catholic Church.

Dominic Barberi

SCRUPLES

Fly from scruples as from a pestilence; they make the soul lose immense treasures.

Paul of the Cross

SEEING GOD

Seeing God means following Him wherever He might lead.

Gregory of Nyssa

Every little glimpse of God that can be gained exceeds every pain and every joy that man can conceive without it.

Catherine of Genoa

One must see God in everyone.

Catherine Laboure

SEEKING GOD

Lord, You called to me and cried aloud, and You broke through my deafness. You flashed, and shone, and chased away my blindness. You breathed upon me fragrantly; I drew in my breath, and now I pant for You. I tasted, and now I hunger and thirst for You. You touched me, and I burned to enjoy Your peace.

Augustine of Hippo

He alone is God who can never be sought in vain: not even when He cannot be found.

Bernard of Clairvaux

Whenever you seek truth, you seek God, whether or not you know it.

Edith Stein

SELF-CONTROL, TEMPERANCE

Control your tongue and your belly.

Anthony the Great

Those whose will always inclines to self-indulgence refuse to do even what is in their power under the pretext that they have no help from above.

Mark the Ascetic

Let us live soberly. For through our bodily senses, whether we wish it or not, robbers come in. The inside of the house is sure to be blackened when the smoke that is climbing up the outer walls finds the windows open.

Amma Syncletice

He who obeys not the rudder will obey the reef.

Herve of Brittany

Temperance is simply a disposition of the mind that sets bounds to the passions.

Thomas Aquinas

SELF-KNOWLEDGE

That you may be able to know God, first know yourself.

Cyprian of Carthage

Whenever we sit in the hairdresser's chair to have our hair cut, we take the mirror and carefully examine the arrangement of every lock.... Yet of our soul, deformed and transformed into a wild beast ... we haven't even the least perception.

John Chrysostom

O Lord my God ... in Your sight I have become a riddle to myself.

Augustine of Hippo

In other living creatures the ignorance of themselves is natural, but in men it is vice.

Severinus

Dwell in the cell of self-knowledge in order to know God's goodness.

Catherine of Siena

The truth is, we never really know ourselves.

Teresa of Avila

Wouldn't it show great ignorance ... if someone when asked who he was didn't know, and didn't know his father or mother or from what country he came? Well now, if this would be so extremely stupid, we are incomparably more so when we do not strive to know who we are.

Teresa of Avila

We'll never completely know ourselves if we don't strive to know God. By gazing at His grandeur, we encounter our own lowliness; by looking at His purity, we see our own filth; by thinking on His humility, we see how far we are from being humble.

Teresa of Avila

You persist in being worldly, superficial, scatterbrained ... because you are a coward. What is it but cowardice not to want to face yourself?

Josemaria Escriva

SELF-WILL

Our self-will is so subtle and so deeply rooted within us, so covered with excuses and defended by false reasoning, that it seems to be a demon. When we cannot do our own will in one way, we do it in another, under all kinds of pretexts.

Catherine of Genoa

SERVICE TO GOD

We have to serve God in His way, not in ours.

Teresa of Avila

If we wish to make any progress in the service of God, we must begin every day of our life with new ardor.

Charles Cardinal Borromeo

What does it matter to a truly loving soul whether God be served by this means or by another?

Francis de Sales

There is nothing small in the service of God.

Francis de Sales

God has created me to do Him some definite service; He has committed some work to me which He has not committed to another. I have my mission—I never may know it in this life, but I shall be told it in the next.

John Henry Cardinal Newman

SICKNESS

In the same way that a powerful medicine cures an illness, so illness itself is a medicine to cure passion. And there is much profit of soul in bearing illness quietly and giving thanks to God.

Amma Syncletice

When we are sick, then we begin truly to know ourselves; then pain brings us home to ourselves; then we think how merry a thing it would be to pray in good health, though we can't do that now because of our grief.... Then we think within ourselves, that if ever we recover and mend in body, we will amend in soul, leave all vices, and be virtuously occupied for the rest of our life. For that reason, we should be, when we are healthy, as we think we would be when we are sick.

Thomas More

When the Lord knows that good health is necessary for our welfare, He sends it to us; and when we need sickness, He sends that too.

Teresa of Avila

Make sickness itself a prayer.

Francis de Sales

The prayer of the sick person is his patience and his acceptance of his sickness for the love of Jesus Christ.

Charles of Sezze

Truly sickness is a great God-given grace. It makes us discover who we are.

Paul of the Cross

Regarding a grave illness:
He who has made me, unmakes me.

Eugenie Smet

SILENCE

He accomplishes more by his silence than others that talk to no purpose.

Ignatius of Antioch

Silence is a gift of God, to let us speak more intimately with Him.

Vincent Pallotti

SIMPLICITY

Be sober and hard-working men; avoid all vanity of dress that will exclude you from heaven; try to keep to the simplicity of manners of our fathers.

Nicholas of Flue

Craftiness is the accumulation of artifices, intrigues, deceits, and appearances to mislead the minds of those with whom we converse. This is quite the reverse of simplicity, which requires that the outside should correspond with what is inside.

Francis de Sales

God in His nature is most simple and cannot admit of any duplicity. If we then would be conformed to Him, we should try to become by virtue what He is by nature. We should be simple in our affections, intentions, actions, and words; we should do what we find to do without artifice or guile, being on the outside what we are on the inside.

Vincent de Paul

I detest dissimulation. What I have in my heart I have also on my tongue.

Paul of the Cross

SIN, SINS

What leper, when he has been healed, turns again and desires to have his leprosy back? You have put off your transgressions in baptism—forsake them!

Ephraem the Syrian

The end of sin is death.

Basil the Great

Committing sin estranges us from God and puts us in league with the Devil.

Basil the Great

The condemnation of those who know and yet do not apply their knowledge is the more severe; but even sin committed in ignorance is not without risk.

Basil the Great

Whoever is drawn into sin against his will should understand that, because he allowed himself to be mastered by another sin committed previously, he is now, as a consequence of this first sin, led into another against his will.

Basil the Great

Often God gives a man over to evil works as punishment for his past deeds of wickedness.

Basil the Great

Sins that are easiest to amend bring the greatest punishment.

John Chrysostom

Prosperous sinners fare worst of all in the end.

John Chrysostom

There is only one thing to be feared ... only one trial, and that is sin.... All the rest is beside the point, whether you talk of plots, feuds, betrayals, slanders, abuses, accusations, confiscations of property, exile, sharpened swords, open sea, or universal war. Whatever they may be, they are all fugitive and they will perish. They touch the mortal body, but wreak no harm on the watchful soul.

John Chrysostom

The sinner is not cast out; he casts himself out.

Ambrose of Milan

We avoid the eyes of men to commit sin, yet we do it in God's presence.

Ambrose of Milan

Sin for man is a disorder and perversion: that is, a turning away from the most worthy Creator and a turning toward the inferior things that He has created.

Augustine of Hippo

Sins, however great and detestable they may be, are looked upon as trivial, or not as sins at all, when men get accustomed to them; and so far does this go, that such sins are not only not concealed, but are boasted of, and published far and wide.... In our own times, many forms of sin ... are now so openly and habitually practiced that we dare not excommunicate a layman, we dare not even defrock a clergyman, for the commission of them.

Augustine of Hippo

Every sin is more harmful to the sinner than to the one sinned against.

Augustine of Hippo

All sin is a kind of lying.

Augustine of Hippo

We may not sin in order to prevent someone else from sinning.

Augustine of Hippo

A sin that is not quickly blotted out by repentance is both a sin and a cause of sin.

Pope Gregory the Great

Sin becomes much more scandalous when the sinner is honored for his position.

Pope Gregory the Great

The goodness of God knows how to use our disordered wishes and actions, often lovingly turning them to our advantage while always preserving the beauty of His order.

Bernard of Clairvaux

To sin is nothing else than not to render God His due.

Anselm of Canterbury

The life of sin is a fall from coherence into chaos; the life of virtue a climb from the many to the One.

Thomas Aquinas

The body of a sinner is a tomb, covering a soul dead by sin.

Thomas Aquinas

There are two sides to every sin: the turning of the will toward fleeting satisfaction and the turning away from everlasting value. As regards the first, the principle of all sins can be called lust—lust in its most general sense, namely, the unbridled desire for one's own pleasure. As regards the second, the principle is pride—pride in its general sense, the lack of submission to God.

Thomas Aquinas

To sin is human, but to persist in sin is devilish.

Catherine of Siena

The Devil's primary enterprise and proudest triumph consists in the bringing of a man to abuse that thing which is best in his own nature.

Thomas More

Among all the circumstances surrounding an evil deed it is hard to find one more hateful to God than the perversion of the real nature of good things to make them into instruments of our malice.

Thomas More

Just as water extinguishes fire, so love wipes away sin.

John of God

Sin is a cruel murder, a frightful act of God-murder, a ghastly annihilation of all things. It is murder because it is the only cause of death, both of the body and of the soul of man. It is God-murder because sin and the sinner caused Christ to die on the cross, and the sinner continues this crucifixion of Jesus, day by day, within himself.

John Eudes

We have only one evil to fear, and that is sin.

Alphonsus Liguori

One must deal with some sinners as with snails: Put them first in cool water until they come out, and then cook them little by little before they realize what's happening to them.

Anthony Mary Claret

Enjoy yourself as much as you like—if only you keep from sin.

John Bosco

Don't imitate those who deceive themselves by saying, "I will sin and then go to confession." How do you know that you will have time to make your confession? Isn't it madness to wound yourself, in the hope that a doctor will be found to heal the wound?

John Bosco

Guard your eyes, since they are the windows through which sin enters the soul.

John Bosco

Death, but not sin!

Dominic Savio

SIN, MORTAL

We should all realize that no matter where or how a man dies, if he is in the state of mortal sin and does not repent, when he could have done so and did not, the Devil tears his soul from his body with such anguish and distress that only a person who has experienced it can appreciate it.

Francis of Assisi

To her son, King St. Louis IX:
Rather would I see you dead at my feet than stained with a mortal sin.

Queen Blanche of France

You should permit yourself to be tormented by every kind of martyrdom before you would allow yourself to commit a mortal sin.

King Louis IX of France

Even if you are committing mortal sins, keep on praying, and I guarantee that you will reach the harbor of salvation.

Teresa of Avila

SINGING, SONG

To sing is to pray twice.

Augustine of Hippo

To sing is the work of a lover.

Augustine of Hippo

Song is the leap of mind in the eternal breaking out into sound.

Thomas Aquinas

The soul of one who serves God always swims in joy, always keeps holiday, and is always in the mood for singing.

John of the Cross

SINNERS

We should not bear with sinners in silence.

Basil the Great

We should tolerate association with sinners only for the purpose of recalling them to repentance, by every means short of committing sin ourselves. But when every form of solicitude has been applied in their regard, we should avoid those who persist in their evil ways.

Basil the Great

With love of the sinner, hatred of the sin.

Augustine of Hippo

SISTERS — *See Religious Life; Virgins, Consecrated*

SLAVES, SLAVERY

The peculiar characteristic of slavery is to be always in fear.

Ambrose of Milan

He who is kind is free, even if he is a slave; he who is evil is a slave, even if he is a king.

Augustine of Hippo

SOLDIER, THE CHRISTIAN AS

Train hard together: wrestle together, run together, suffer together, rest together, rise together, as stewards in God's house, members of His household, and His servants. Win the approval of the One in whose ranks you serve and from whom you draw your pay. Let none of you turn deserter. Let your baptism be your arms; your faith, your helmet; your love, your spear; your endurance, your armor. Let your good works be your deposits from your soldier's wages, so that you may receive back all that you have been careful to save.

Ignatius of Antioch

Refusing further service as a Roman soldier:
I am a soldier of Christ: combat is not permitted to me.

Martin of Tours

In Confirmation ... we are enrolled by bishops, who are like the leaders in Christ's army; the imposition of hands reminds us that virtue and strength come from Christ.

Thomas Aquinas

What, then, does God watch with pleasure and delight? The man who is fighting for Him against riches, against the world, against hell, against himself.

Louis de Montfort

SOLITUDE

Believe one who has tried: You shall find a fuller satisfaction in the woods than in books. The trees and the rocks will teach you what you cannot hear from the masters.

Bernard of Clairvaux

It is good when a soul loves solitude; it's a sign that it takes delight in God and enjoys speaking with Him.

Jane Frances de Chantal

Aim at a great interior nakedness, poverty of spirit: keep yourself in true interior solitude, in the depth of essence of the soul, which is the same as saying: remain in the temple of your soul.

Paul of the Cross

You have to cast yourself into the abyss of that divine solitude. Love and be silent, be silent and love! What silence, what sacred silence, what deep and holy love!

Paul of the Cross

SORROW — *See also Affliction; Trials*

Sorrow is given us on purpose to cure us of sin.

John Chrysostom

O Lord, You who use sorrow to teach, and wound us to heal, and kill us lest we die to You!

Augustine of Hippo

Sorrow can be alleviated by good sleep, a bath, and a glass of wine.

Thomas Aquinas

All the joys of this life are accompanied by sorrows: if they were not, we would grow too much absorbed in them.

Teresa of Avila

No picture can be drawn with only the brightest colors, nor harmony created only from treble notes.... Our whole life is tempered between sweet and sour, and we must look for a mixture of both.

Robert Southwell

THE SOUL

Know that this soul of yours is free, self-determining, the fairest work of God, made according to the image of its Creator, immortal because of God who makes it immortal, a living being, rational, imperishable, because of Him who has conferred these gifts; having power to do as it will.

Cyril of Jerusalem

He has not only delivered us from sins, but has made us lovable. Just as if someone were to take a leper consumed by illness and disease, and by age and poverty and hunger, and were to turn him suddenly into a handsome youth surpassing all men by his beauty, shedding a bright sunbeam from his cheeks, yes, shaming the dazzling beams of the sun with the sparkle of his eyes; and then were to set him down in the flower of his age, and on top of that, array him in purple and a diadem and all the royal regalia: That is how God has decked out our soul, how beautiful and desirable and lovable He has made it.

John Chrysostom

Each soul is in itself a world of God, and each one voyages within His own heart; nor is he shipwrecked, if he dwells on the things that are worthy.

Augustine of Hippo

The soul is the inner face of man, by which we are known, that we may be regarded with love by our Maker.

Pope Gregory the Great

Every holy soul is itself a heaven in a sense—a heaven with understanding for its sun, faith for its moon, and virtues for its stars, a heaven where God dwells, according to His faithful promise.

Bernard of Clairvaux

Understanding and love—that is, the knowledge of and delight in the truth—are, as it were, the two arms of the soul, with which it embraces and comprehends with all saints the length and breadth, the height and depth, that is, the eternity, the love, the goodness, and the wisdom of God.

Bernard of Clairvaux

We know we have souls. But we seldom consider the precious things that can be found in this soul, or who dwells within it, or its high value. Consequently, little effort is made to preserve its beauty. All our attention is taken up with the plainness of the diamond's setting ... that is, with these bodies of ours.

Teresa of Avila

I knew well that I had a soul; but I did not understand the dignity of this soul, nor did I know who lodged within it, because my eyes were blinded by the vanities of this life, so that I was prevented from seeing Him. I think that, had I known then as I do now, that in this little palace of my soul so great a King is lodged, I would not have left Him alone so often, but at least sometimes I would have stayed with Him and been more careful to prepare a clean lodging for Him.

Teresa of Avila

God dwells in a secret and hidden way in all souls, in their very substance, for if He did not, they could not exist at all.

John of the Cross

All the world together is not worth one soul.

Francis de Sales

SPEECH

When you love unseemly conversation, you prepare a feast for demons.

Ephraem the Syrian

Let your speech be brief and savory.

Ephraem the Syrian

If you mock your fellow, you are the mouth of the devil.... A spacious dwelling for Satan is the man that mocks his neighbor; a palace of the enemy is the heart of the mocker.

Ephraem the Syrian

For a Christian, a promise is a debt.

Cyril of Jerusalem

When you speak evil, even if it is true, that is still a crime.

John Chrysostom

Happy the man whose words issue from the Holy Spirit and not from himself.

Anthony of Padua

No idle word should be uttered. I understand a word to be idle when it serves no good purpose, either for myself or for another, and was not intended to do so.

Ignatius Loyola

In all talking and conversation let something always be said of spiritual things, and so shall all idle words and evil speaking be avoided.

Teresa of Avila

Never utter in your neighbor's absence what you wouldn't say in his presence.

Mary Magdalene dei Pazzi

Avoid those who in your presence aren't ashamed to make use of scandalous words and double entendres.

John Bosco

SPIRITUAL DIRECTORS

Receive counsel in everything you do, and you won't be sorry when you've done it.

Benedict of Nursia

He who wants to stand alone without the support of a master and guide will be like the tree that stands alone in a field without a caretaker. No matter how much the tree bears, passers-by will pick the fruit before it ripens.

John of the Cross

The virtuous soul that is alone and without a master is like a lone burning coal; it will grow colder rather than hotter.

John of the Cross

When the enemy of our human nature tempts a righteous soul with his deceits and seductions, he earnestly desires that they be received in secret and kept secret. But if we manifest them to a confessor, or to some other spiritual person who understands his wiles and malicious intentions, the evil one is quite vexed. He knows that he cannot succeed in his evil endeavor, once his evident tricks have been revealed.

Ignatius Loyola

Would you walk in earnest toward devotion? Seek some good man who will guide you; this is the greatest of all words of advice.

Francis de Sales

There are so many souls that would attain sanctity if only they were well directed.

Thérèse of Lisieux

SPIRITUAL DISCIPLINES, SPIRITUAL EXERCISES

Discipline, the safeguard of hope, the bond of faith, the guide of the way of salvation, the stimulus and nourishment of good dispositions, the teacher of virtue, causes us to abide always in Christ, and to live continually for God, and to attain to the heavenly promises and to the divine rewards. To follow her is wholesome, and to turn away from her and neglect her is deadly.

Cyprian of Carthage

Solitude, vigils in the night, manual labor, nakedness, reading, and the other disciplines—we know that their purpose is to free the heart from injury by bodily passions and to keep it free; they are to be the rungs of a ladder up which it may climb to perfect love. If by accident some right and needful occupation prevents us from keeping these acts of discipline, we should not be guilty of gloom or annoyance—for the aim of these acts is to drive away such faults.... None of these practices are of any profit at all if the purpose for which they are undertaken is lost.

Moses the Black

Just as taking a walk, journeying on foot, and running are bodily exercises, so we call "spiritual exercises" every way of preparing and disposing the soul to rid itself of all inordinate attachments, and, after their removal, of seeking and finding the will of God in the disposition of our life for the salvation of our soul.

Ignatius Loyola

SPIRITUAL GIFTS

A man might seem to confess the Lord and hear His words, yet if he does not obey the Lord's commands, he is condemned—even if, by some divine concession, he is vouchsafed an endowment of spiritual gifts.

Basil the Great

SPIRITUAL GROWTH

Let us imitate what we shall one day be.

Cyprian of Carthage

Even as a man just recovered from an illness walks on his journey only as far as is absolutely necessary, and then with pain and difficulty, so the repentant sinner treads in God's ways heavily and slowly until, having attained the grace of devotion, he resembles the healthy and light-hearted traveler, who not only proceeds on his way, but runs and leaps with joy in the way of God's commandments, hastening into the paths of His heavenly counsels and aspirations.

Francis de Sales

SUFFERING

Life Himself came down to be slain; Bread came down to suffer hunger; the Way came down to endure weariness on His journey; the Fountain came down to experience thirst. Do you, then, refuse to work and to suffer?

Augustine of Hippo

God said: Why do you never stop asking to taste of My delights, yet you refuse the tribulations?

Margaret of Cortona

Suffering is a short pain and a long joy.

Henry Suso

If God causes you to suffer much, it's a sign that He has great designs for you, and that He certainly intends to make you a saint.

Ignatius Loyola

Suffering out of love for God is better than working miracles.

John of the Cross

The purest suffering bears and carries in its train the purest understanding.

John of the Cross

One must not think that a person who is suffering is not praying. He is offering up his sufferings to God, and many a time he is praying much more truly than one who goes away by himself and meditates his head off, and, if he has squeezed out a few tears, thinks that is prayer.

Teresa of Avila

Blessed be He, who came into the world for no other purpose than to suffer.

Teresa of Avila

Suffering is a great favor. Remember that everything soon comes to an end ... and take courage. Think of how our gain is eternal.

Teresa of Avila

The greatness of our God must be tested by the desire we have of suffering for His sake.

Philip Neri

Surely nothing is too much for Him when there is a question of sanctifying a soul. He hands over the body and soul to weakness in order to purify them in contempt of earthly things and in the love of His Majesty. He wounds and He heals them; He crucifies them on His cross in order to glorify them in His glory; in short, He gives them death in order to have them live in eternity. Let us accept these appearances of evil in order to have the real goods they produce, and we will be happy both in this life and in the next.

Vincent de Paul

Suffer and offer up those trifling injuries, those petty inconveniences, that daily befall you—this toothache, this headache, this cold, this contempt or scorn.

Francis de Sales

Suffering borne in the will quietly and patiently is a continual, very power-ful prayer before God.

Jane Frances de Chantal

The more we suffer, the more we are favored by God.

Jane Frances de Chantal

Without misfortune, you might not have been wholly bad, but perhaps you might not have been entirely good, either.

Claude de la Colombiere

When it is all over, you will not regret having suffered; rather you will regret having suffered so little, and suffered that little so badly.

Sebastian Valfre

Do as the merchant does with his merchandise: Make a profit on every item. Don't allow the loss of the tiniest fragment of the true cross. It may be only the sting of a horsefly or the prick of a pin that annoys you; it may be a neighbor's little eccentricities, some unintended slight, the insignificant loss of a penny, some small restlessness of soul, a light pain in your limbs. Make a profit on every item as the grocer does, and you'll soon be wealthy in God.

Louis de Montfort

I would like to make everyone understand the great grace that God, in His mercy, bestows when He sends suffering, especially suffering devoid of con-solation. Then indeed the soul is purified like gold in the furnace; without knowing it, it becomes radiant and is set free to take flight to its Good.

Paul of the Cross

Those who suffer for the love of God help Jesus carry His cross, and if they persevere they will share His glory in heaven.

Paul of the Cross

Say always, "My beloved and despised Redeemer, how sweet it is to suffer for You."

Alphonsus Liguori

There are people who make capital out of everything, even the winter. If it is cold, they offer their little sufferings to God.

John Vianney

The crosses we meet on the road to heaven are like a fine stone bridge on which you can cross a river. Christians who don't suffer cross this river on a shaky bridge that's always in danger of giving way under their feet.

John Vianney

Once they've been transformed in the flames of love, crosses are like a bundle of hawthorn that you throw on the fire, and that the fire reduces to ashes. The hawthorn is thorny, but the ashes are soft. Hawthorn exudes balm and the cross exudes sweetness. But you've got to press the thorns in your hands and clasp the cross to your heart if you want them to distill the essence they contain.

John Vianney

Can you expect to go to heaven for nothing? Did not our dear Savior track the whole way to it with His tears and blood? And yet you start at every little pain.

Elizabeth Ann Seton

Suffering counts for more than work.

Anthony Mary Claret

As iron is fashioned by the fire and on an anvil, so in the fire of suffering and under the weight of trials, our souls receive the form that our Lord desires for them to have.

Madeleine Sophie Barat

Thank the good God for having visited you through suffering. If we knew the value of suffering, we would ask for it.

Brother Andre Bessette

In reference to our inability at times to find a meaningful pattern in God's actions in our lives:
We see the reverse side of the embroidery, because we are seated on a low stool.

Padre Pio Pietrelcina

God sometimes allows us to be in such a profound darkness that not a single star shines in our skies. The reason is that we must be reminded that we are on earth only to suffer, while following our gentle Savior along a dark and thorny path.

Charles de Foucauld

SUNDAY
It would be the utmost folly for us to give up five and even six days to the business of this life, and yet not to devote so much as one day, or even one small part of a day, to spiritual things.

John Chrysostom

I entreat you, keep Sundays holy. Working on Sunday will not make you rich; on the contrary, you will bring down misfortunes on yourselves and your children.

Bernadette Soubirous

TALKATIVENESS
It's better to keep quiet and be a real Christian than to chatter and not be one.

Ignatius of Antioch

Don't talk too much, not even with words that are wise; for even words that are wise, if they are too many, become wearisome.

Ephraem the Syrian

Remarking on two monks who tended to say the first thing that came into their heads:
Their house has no door. Whoever wants, goes into the stable and steals the donkey.

Antony the Great

Why, you words, did I let you go out? I have often been penitent that I spoke, but never that I kept silent.

Arsenius the Great

How can we guard our heart if our tongue leaves the door of the fortress open?

Sisois

Let your words be few when in the midst of many.

Teresa of Avila

If we say less than we should, it is easy to add; but having said too much, it is hard to take it away.

Francis de Sales

The love of talk distracts all the powers of our soul from God, and fills them with earthly objects and impressions, like a vessel of water which cannot be clear and settled while you are continually stirring the earthy particles from the bottom.

Elizabeth Ann Seton

Speak little to creatures but speak much with God. He will make you truly wise.

Mary Mazarello

TEACHERS, TEACHING

It is good to teach, if the one who teaches also acts.

Ignatius of Antioch

It is dangerous for a man to try teaching before he is trained in the good life. A man whose house is about to fall down may invite travelers inside to refresh them, but instead they are hurt in the collapse of the house. It is the same with teachers who have not carefully trained themselves in the good life: They ruin their hearers as well as themselves. Their mouth invites to salvation, their way of life leads to ruin.

Amma Syncletice

Don't suppose that anyone really learns something from another human being. I can admonish you by the sound of my voice, but if there isn't within you One who teaches, then my words are only meaningless noise.... The instruction that comes from others is a kind of help, a call for attention. But the One who truly teaches the heart teaches from heaven.

Augustine of Hippo

Teaching unsupported by grace may enter our ears, but it never reaches the heart. When God's grace does touch our innermost minds to bring understanding, then His Word, which is received by the ear, can sink deep into the heart.

Isidore of Seville

All who undertake to teach must be endowed with deep love, the greatest patience and, most of all, profound humility. The Lord will find them worthy to become fellow workers with Him in the cause of truth.

Joseph of Calasanza

It is chiefly by asking questions and in provoking explanations that the master must open the mind of the pupil, make him work, and use his thinking powers, form his judgment, and make him find out for himself the answer.

Jean Baptiste de la Salle

Jesus Christ, in His infinite wisdom, used the words and idioms that were in use among those whom He addressed. You should do likewise.

Joseph Cafasso

TEMPTATION

In your strife with the Devil, you have for spectators the angels and the Lord of angels.

Ephraem the Syrian

To those who are just and upright, temptations become helps.

Ephraem the Syrian

As the pilot of a vessel is tried in the storm; as the wrestler is tried in the ring; the soldier in the battle, and the hero in adversity: so is the Christian tried in temptation.

Basil the Great

When we are tempted to utter a sinful word, or when we find ourselves being carried away by anger or some other such passion, let us reflect on what privileges we have been granted, what Spirit it is whose presence we enjoy, and this thought will check in us those unruly passions.

John Chrysostom

The Devil tempts so that he may ruin; God tempts so that He may crown.

Ambrose of Milan

For the Devil does not seduce or influence anyone, unless he finds him ready in some part similar to himself. He finds him coveting something, and greed opens the door for the Devil's suggestion to enter.

Augustine of Hippo

The tempter, ever on the lookout, wages war most violently against those whom he sees most careful to avoid sin.

Pope Leo the Great

Close your ears to the whisperings of hell and bravely oppose its onslaughts.

Clare of Assisi

He did not say: You will not be troubled—you will not be tempted—you will not be distressed. But He said: You will not be overcome.

Julian of Norwich

All the temptations of hell cannot stain a soul that does not love them.

Francis de Sales

It is not always in the soul's power not to feel a temptation. But it is always in its power not to consent to it.

Francis de Sales

THANKSGIVING, GRATITUDE TO GOD

We must take to heart, brothers, from what stuff we were created, who we were and what kind of creatures we were when we entered the world, as if from a tomb and from utter darkness. Having prepared for us bountifully before we were born, He who fashioned us and created us brought us into His world. Since, then, we owe all this to Him, we ought to give Him thanks for everything.

Pope Clement I

Be eager for more frequent gatherings for thanksgiving to God and His glory. For when we meet in this way, the forces of Satan are rendered powerless and his destructive power is canceled in the concord of your faith.

Ignatius of Antioch

When you lie down on your bed, remember with thanksgiving the blessings and the providence of God.

Antony the Great

We should not accept in silence the benefactions of God, but return thanks for them.

Basil the Great

Thanking is a new, inward knowing, with great reverence and loving awe.

Julian of Norwich

One act of thanksgiving when things go wrong with us is worth a thousand thanks when things are agreeable to our inclination.

John of Avila

In all created things discern the providence and wisdom of God, and in all things give Him thanks.

Teresa of Avila

If we have any natural defect, either in mind or body, let us not grieve and be sorry for ourselves. Who is there that ever receives a gift and tries to make bargains about it? Let us, then, return thanks for what He has bestowed on us. Who can tell whether, if we had had a larger share of ability or stronger health, we would have possessed them to our destruction?

Alphonsus Liguori

Alas, yet if I am not one of His elect, it is only I to be blamed, and when *going down* [to hell] I must still lift the hands to the very last look in praise and gratitude for what He has done to save me. What more could He have done?

Elizabeth Ann Seton

THEOLOGY

The purpose of theology is threefold: to refute error, to teach sound morals, and to contemplate truth.

Thomas Aquinas

Love is the abridgment of all theology.

Francis de Sales

THEOLOGY, INNOVATIONS IN

Let them innovate in nothing, but keep the traditions.

Pope Stephen I

"Guard," says [the Apostle Paul], "what has been committed" [1 Tim 6:20]. What does it mean?... It is what has been faithfully entrusted to you, not what has been discovered by you; what you have received, not what you have thought up; a matter not of ingenuity, but of doctrine; not of private acquisition, but of public Tradition; a matter brought to you, not put forth by you, in which you must not be the author but the guardian, not the founder but the sharer, not the leader, but the follower.

Vincent of Lerins

THEOLOGY, SPECULATIONS IN

To ask questions such as these, and to make such guesses as we can at the answers, is a useful exercise for the intellect, if the discussion be kept within proper bounds, and if we avoid the error of supposing ourselves to know what we do not know. For what is the necessity of affirming, or denying, or defining with accuracy on these subjects, when we may without blame be entirely ignorant of them?

Augustine of Hippo

THOUGHT, THOUGHTS

Thoughts inevitably besiege the mind. But any earnest person has the power to accept or reject them. Their origin is in some ways outside ourselves, but whether to choose them or not lies within us.

Moses the Black

Just as you cannot stop air from coming into your chest, you cannot stop evil thoughts from coming into your mind. Your part is to resist them.

Abba Poemen

If you shut a snake or a scorpion in a box, in the end it will die. And wicked thoughts that the demons scatter slowly lose their power if the victim has endurance.

Abba Poemen

Men have the power of thinking so that they may avoid sin.

John Chrysostom

Thought is a kind of sight of the mind.

Augustine of Hippo

Occupy your minds with good thoughts, or the enemy will fill them with bad ones. Unoccupied, they cannot be.

Thomas More

In thought, there are two ways of sinning mortally. The first is to consent to the evil thought with the intention of carrying it out, or of doing so if one can. The second way of sinning mortally is actually carrying out the sin to which consent was given.

Ignatius Loyola

If any bad thought comes to you, make the sign of the cross, or say an Our Father, or strike your breast, and try to think of something else. If you do that, the thought will actually be winning you merit, because you will be resisting it.

Teresa of Avila

A single human thought is worth more than the whole world; hence, God alone is worthy of being its subject.

John of the Cross

TIME, RIGHT USE OF

A Christian is not his own master, since all his time belongs to God.

Ignatius of Antioch

Time takes no holidays.

Augustine of Hippo

Do now—do *now*—what you'll wish you had done when your moment comes to die.

Angela Merici

Since, when the hour of reckoning comes, you'll be sorry for not having used this time in the service of God, why don't you arrange and use it now as you would wish you'd done if you were dying?

John of the Cross

When death comes, the mighty messenger of God, no king can command him, no authority can restrain him, no riches can hire him to wait past his appointed time even one moment of an hour. Therefore let us consider well in time what words we are bound to speak and what deeds we are bound to do, and let us say them and do them quickly. And let us leave unsaid and undone all superfluous things (and, much more, all damnable things), knowing well that we have no empty time allowed to us.

Thomas More

THE TIMES

"These are bad times," people are saying, "troublesome times!" If only our lives were all good, our times would be good, for we ourselves make our times—as we are, so are our times. But what can we do? After all, we cannot convert the mass of humanity to a good life. But let the few who do listen to the will of God live good lives; and let the few who live good lives endure the many who do not. The good are the wheat, still on the threshing floor; and though the chaff lies with them there, the chaff will not come with them to the barn.

Augustine of Hippo

Truly, matters in the world are in a bad state; but if you and I begin in earnest to reform ourselves, a really good beginning will have been made.

Peter of Alcantara

TRADITION

Even if the apostles had not left their writings to us, ought we not to follow the rule of the tradition that they handed down to those to whom they committed the churches?

Irenaeus of Lyons

It is needful also to make use of Tradition, for not everything can be gotten from sacred Scripture. The holy Apostles handed down some things in the Scriptures, other things in Tradition.

Epiphanius of Salamis

Of the dogmas and preaching preserved in the Church, some we possess from written teaching and others we receive from the tradition of the Apostles, handed on to us in mystery. In respect to piety, both are of the same force.

Basil the Great

"Therefore, brethren, stand fast and hold the traditions that you have been taught, whether by word or by our letter" [2 Th 2:15]. From this it is clear that they did not hand down everything by letter, but there was much also that was not written. Like that which was written, the unwritten too is worthy of belief. So let us regard the tradition of the Church also as worthy of belief. Is it a tradition? Inquire no further.

John Chrysostom

Keep the talent of the Catholic faith inviolate and unimpaired. What has been faithfully entrusted, let it remain in your possession, let it be handed on by you. You have received gold, so give gold. For my part, I do not want you to substitute one thing for another; I do not want you impudently to put lead in place of gold, or, fraudulently, brass. I do not want the appearance of gold, but the real thing.

Vincent of Lerins

A small thing is not small when it leads to something great; and it is no small matter to forsake the ancient tradition of the Church that was upheld by all those who were called before us, whose conduct we should observe, and whose faith we should imitate.

John of Damascus

A single opinion cannot overturn the unanimous tradition of the whole Church, which has spread to the end of the earth.

John of Damascus

We do not advocate one thing at one time and change it at another; otherwise the faith would become a joke to those outside.

John of Damascus

TRIALS — *See also Afflictions; Sorrow*

In the midst of adversities, I desire prosperous days; in the midst of prosperity, I dread adversity. Between these two, is there no middle ground where the life of man is not a trial?

Augustine of Hippo

I pray God may open your eyes and let you see what hidden treasures He bestows on us in the trials from which the world thinks only to flee.

John of Avila

We always find that those who walked closest to Christ, our Lord, were those who had to bear the greatest trials.

Teresa of Avila

Since gold and silver, which are only corruptible metals, are purified and tested by fire, it is but reasonable that our faith, which surpasses all the riches of the world, should be tried.

Peter Claver

God wishes to test you like gold in the furnace. The dross is consumed by the fire, but the pure gold remains and its value increases.

Jerome Emiliani

TRINITY, THE MOST HOLY

I believe in one God, the Source of all things, without beginning, uncreated, immortal and unassailable, eternal, everlasting, incomprehensible, bodiless, invisible, uncircumscribed, without form. I believe in one superessential Being, one Godhead greater than our conception of divinity, in three Persons: Father, Son, and Holy Spirit, and I adore Him alone. I worship one God, one Godhead, but I adore three Persons: God the Father, God the Son made flesh, and God the Holy Spirit, one God.

John of Damascus

The high might of the Trinity is our father, and the deep wisdom of the Trinity is our mother, and the great love of the Trinity is our Lord.

Julian of Norwich

TRUST IN GOD

All shall be well, and all shall be well, and all manner of things shall be well.

Julian of Norwich

I am afraid that if we begin to put our trust in human help, some of our Divine help will fail us.

Teresa of Avila

Consider seriously how quickly people change, and how little trust is to be had in them; and hold fast to God, who does not change.

Teresa of Avila

We shall steer safely through every storm, as long as our heart is right, our intention fervent, our courage steadfast, and our trust fixed in God.

Francis de Sales

The past must be abandoned to God's mercy, the present to our faithfulness, the future to divine providence.

Francis de Sales

Entrust yourself entirely to God. He is a Father and a most loving Father at that, who would rather let heaven and earth collapse than abandon anyone who trusted in Him.

Paul of the Cross

With the confidence of a son, rest in the care and love that divine Providence has for you in all your needs. Look upon Providence as a child does its mother who loves him tenderly. You can be sure that God loves you incomparably more.

Jane Frances de Chantal

Whatever good or evil befalls you, be confident that God will convert it all to your good.

Jane Frances de Chantal

The more you abandon to God the care of all temporal things, the more He will take care to provide for all your wants; but if, on the contrary, you try to supply all your own needs, Providence will allow you to continue to do just that, and then it may very well happen that even necessities will be lacking, God thus reproving you for your lack of faith and reliance on Him.

Jean Baptiste de la Salle

He who trusts in himself is lost. He who trusts in God can do all things.

Alphonsus Liguori

Whatever, wherever I am, I can never be thrown away. If I am in sickness, my sickness may serve Him; if I am in sorrow, my sorrow may serve Him.... He does nothing in vain; He may prolong my life, He may shorten it; He knows what He is about. He may take away my friends, He may throw me among strangers, He may make me feel desolate, make my spirits sink, hide the future from me—still He knows what He is about.

John Henry Cardinal Newman

I have started houses with no more than the price of a loaf of bread and prayers, for with Him who comforts me, I can do anything.

Frances Xavier Cabrini

The heart of God invites all to put it to the proof. The more He gives, the more He desires to give. He loves to see the trust that makes us persist in knocking unceasingly.

Placid Riccardi

TRUTH

All truth, wherever it is found, belongs to us as Christians.

Justin Martyr

No one is truly poor but except the one who lacks the truth.

Ephraem the Syrian

Truth is one; contradictions of the truth are manifold.

Cyril of Jerusalem

Those who wage war against the truth are powerless to win; rather, they wound themselves, like those who kick against spikes.

John Chrysostom

We must have such great love for the truth that our words will take on the character of oaths.

Paulinus of Nola

I invoke You, O God, the Truth—in whom and from whom and through whom all things are true that anywhere are true.

Augustine of Hippo

Nothing conquers except truth; the victory of truth is charity.

Augustine of Hippo

People hate the truth for the sake of whatever it is they love more than the truth. They love truth when it shines warmly on them, and hate it when it rebukes them.

Augustine of Hippo

O God of truth, I seek that I may receive, so that my joy may be full. Till then, let my mind meditate on it, and let my tongue speak of it; let my heart love it, and the words of my mouth be about it.

Anselm of Canterbury

Truth is the identity of thought and thing.

Thomas Aquinas

What God's Son has told me, I take for truth. Truth Himself speaks truly, or else there is nothing true.

Thomas Aquinas

Every truth without exception—no matter who may utter it—is from the Holy Spirit.

Thomas Aquinas

Truth suffers, but never dies.

Teresa of Avila

In Him, therefore, do I understand and possess all truth that is in heaven and earth and hell, and in all creatures; and so great is the truth and the certainty that were the whole world to declare the contrary, I would not believe it—indeed, I would mock it.

Angela of Foligno

Those who are led by the Holy Spirit have true ideas; that's why so many ignorant people are wiser than the learned.

John Vianney

Truth is one; therefore ... the multitude of men are wrong, as far as they differ; and as they differ, not about trivial points, but about great matters, it follows that the multitude of men, whether by their own fault or not, are wrong even in the greater matters of religion.

John Henry Cardinal Newman

Error may flourish for a time, but truth will prevail in the end. The only effect of error ultimately is to promote truth.

John Henry Cardinal Newman

Chosen by himself to be written on his gravestone:
From shadows and symbols to the truth.

John Henry Cardinal Newman

UNBELIEF, UNBELIEVERS

Let no one be deceived: Even the heavenly beings, the splendor of the angels, the principalities, both seen and unseen, if they fail to believe in the blood of Christ, are damned.

Ignatius of Antioch

There are two kinds of coins, one God's, the other the world's. Each bears its own stamp: unbelievers that of this world; believers, who are spurred by love, the stamp of God the Father through Jesus Christ.

Ignatius of Antioch

These days no one thinks of the fears that the future holds; no one takes to heart the day of judgment, and the wrath of God; the punishments to come upon unbelievers, and the eternal torments decreed for the faithless. Whatever a conscience would fear if it believed, our conscience, because it no longer believes, doesn't fear at all. If only it believed, it would take heed; and if it took heed, it would escape.

Cyprian of Carthage

No one is so foolish as not to believe that the things of the physical world are subject to someone's government, providence, and disposition, seeing that they are regulated according to a certain order and time. Thus we see the sun, the moon, and the stars and other parts of the physical world all holding a certain course, which would not happen if they were the sport of chance. For that reason, a man would be a fool not to believe in God.

Thomas Aquinas

Unbelievers call themselves rational; not because they decide by evidence, but because, after they have made their decision, they merely occupy themselves in sifting it.

John Henry Cardinal Newman

UNITY, CHRISTIAN

Your accord and harmonious love is a hymn to Jesus Christ. Yes, you should form all together one choir, so that, in perfect harmony and taking your pitch from God, you may sing with one voice to the Father through Jesus Christ, that He may listen to you and know you from your chant as the canticle of His only Son.

Ignatius of Antioch

The time will come when there will be one flock and one shepherd, one faith and one clear knowledge of God.

Bridget of Sweden

UNIVERSE

The entire universe pre-exists in the Godhead, which is its primordial cause. Father, Son, and Holy Spirit are all in all, because in their divinity every other thing is anticipated and possessed.

Thomas Aquinas

The entire universe is one dominion and realm, governed by one Ruler, who is the First Mover, the First Truth, the First Good—God, blessed forever and ever.

Thomas Aquinas

God is an artist, and the universe is His work of art.

Thomas Aquinas

USURY

Nothing, nothing is baser than the usury of this world, nothing more cruel. Why, such a man traffics in the calamities of others; he makes himself gains from others' distress; he demands wages for kindness as though he were afraid to seem merciful. Under the cloak of kindness he digs the pitfall deeper; by his help, he galls a man's poverty; in the act of stretching out a hand, he thrusts him down; and when receiving him in harbor, he sends him to shipwreck.

John Chrysostom

VAINGLORY

We should let God be the One to praise us and not praise ourselves. For God detests those who commend themselves. Let others applaud our good deeds.

Pope Clement I

If you put wax in front of a fire, it melts; and if you pour vain praises on the soul, it goes soft and weak in seeking goodness.

Amma Syncletice

If you glory in yourself and not in the Lord, you will be kissing your own hand instead of the hand of your Benefactor.

Bernard of Clairvaux

The desire to be well-thought-of—what is it other than a desire for different treatment from what was accorded to the Son of God? How was He content to be regarded by the people? As a madman, a rebel, a fool, a sinner.... Vanity shoots up and will grow strong if we do not crush it and look solely for the glory of God, for which only we must work.

Vincent de Paul

To prefer man to God: a strange and unhappy slavery is that of a man who seeks to please other men.... I vow never to do anything nor to leave anything undone because of what people think.... It will set up in me a great interior peace.

Claude de la Colombiere

VICE, VICES

Vice mimics virtue.

Cyril of Jerusalem

This is the definition of vice: the wrong use, in violation of the Lord's commandment, of what has been given us by God for a good purpose.

Basil the Great

We make a ladder of our vices when we trample them underfoot.

Augustine of Hippo

Vice is contrary to human nature, because it is against the order of reason.

Thomas Aquinas

When we are assailed by some vice we must, as far as possible, embrace the practice of the contrary virtue.

Francis de Sales

VICTORY IN CHRIST

The crown of victory is promised only to those who engage in the struggle.

Augustine of Hippo

You can fight with confidence when you are sure of victory. With Christ and for Christ, victory is certain.

Bernard of Clairvaux

VIRGINS, CONSECRATED

Virgins ... are the flowers of the Church, the beauty and ornament of spiritual grace, a subject of joy, a perfect and unsullied homage of praise and honor, the image of God corresponding to the sanctity of the Lord, the most illustrious portion of Christ's flock. In them the glorious fecundity of our mother the Church finds expression, and she rejoices; the more the number of virgins increase, the greater is this mother's joy.

Cyprian of Carthage

A consecrated virgin ought not only to be so, but also to be perceived and believed to be so: No one on seeing a consecrated virgin should be in any doubt as to whether she is one.

Cyprian of Carthage

VIRTUE, THE VIRTUES

The soul feeds on the virtues.

Gregory of Nyssa

Where virtue is, there are many snares.

John Chrysostom

So good a thing is virtue that even its enemies applaud and admire it.

John Chrysostom

Virtue is nothing but well-directed love.

Augustine of Hippo

Virtue makes a good use even of the evils a man suffers.

Augustine of Hippo

No wickedness, no heresy, not even the Devil himself can deceive anyone without counterfeiting virtue.

Dorotheos of Gaza

The essence of virtue consists in the doing of what is good rather than what is difficult.

Thomas Aquinas

O glorious virtue! Who would not give himself to death a thousand times, and endure any suffering through desire, to win you? You are a queen who possesses the entire world; you inhabit the enduring life; for the soul that is arrayed in you is yet mortal, you make it abide by force of love with those who are immortal.

Catherine of Siena

Everyone argues in favor of the virtue he practices easily, and exaggerates the difficulties of the virtues that are contrary to it.

Francis de Sales

True virtue has no limits.

Francis de Sales

In the case of the virtues, sir, it is very easy to pass from defect to excess, from being righteous to being rigorous and rashly zealous. It is said that good wine easily turns to vinegar.

Vincent de Paul

Virtue demands courage, constant effort, and, above all, help from on high.

John Vianney

VOCATION, VOCATIONS

Whoever has been called to the preaching of the Gospel should obey instantly and without delay.

Basil the Great

Each state in life has its special duties; by their accomplishments one may find happiness in the world as well as in solitude; for not all are called to separate themselves from the society of men.

Nicholas of Flue

A good vocation is simply a firm and constant will in which the person who is called must serve God in the way and in the places to which almighty God has called him.

Francis de Sales

If a person shows a firm and persevering determination to serve God in the manner and place to which His divine majesty calls her, she gives the best proof we can have that she has a true vocation.

Francis de Sales

Just as every sort of gem when cast into honey becomes brighter and more sparkling, so each person becomes more acceptable and fitting in his own vocation when he sets that vocation in the context of devotion. Through devotion family cares become more peaceful, mutual love between husband and wife becomes more sincere, the service we owe the prince becomes more faithful, and our work, no matter what it is, becomes more pleasant and agreeable.

Francis de Sales

The grace of even wishing to belong to God must come from Himself.

Elizabeth Ann Seton

Our Lord has created persons for all states in life, and in all of them we see people who have achieved sanctity by fulfilling their obligations well.

Anthony Mary Claret

At last I have found my vocation: My vocation is love.

Thérèse of Lisieux

WAR

For a war to be just, three conditions are necessary: public authority, just cause, right motive.

Thomas Aquinas

WEAKNESS

Your weaknesses and deficiencies ought to make you humble, but you should also throw all of them into the fire of the love of God, where they will be devoured and consumed like a straw mattress thrown into a great furnace.

Paul of the Cross

Consider God's generosity toward you rather than your own unworthiness in His sight, and live in His strength, rather than in thoughts of your own weakness.

Vincent de Paul

WEALTH

You say that you are wealthy and rich, and you think that you should make use of those things that God has willed you should possess. Use them certainly, but for the things of salvation; use them, but for good purposes; use them, but for those things that God has commanded and that the Lord has set forth. Let the poor feel that you are wealthy; let the needy feel that you are rich. Lend your estate to God; give food to Christ.

Cyprian of Carthage

Not everything that *can* be done *ought* to be done.... If you think that God gave you riches for the sole purpose of enjoying them thoroughly yourself—without using them for the purposes of salvation—then you're sinning against God. For God gave us a voice, too, but that doesn't mean we must use it to sing indecent love songs. And God willed that iron be mined from the earth, but not so that we would murder one another with weapons crafted from it.

Cyprian of Carthage

How can they follow Christ when they are held back by the chains of their wealth? Or how can they seek heaven, and climb to sublime and lofty heights, when they are weighed down by earthly desires? They think that they possess, but they themselves are possessed—slaves of their profit; the bond slaves, not the lords, of their own money.

Cyprian of Carthage

The rich man lies awake; his riches chase away his sleep. While his dogs sleep, he guards his treasure from the thieves.

Ephraem the Syrian

Nothing is more false than wealth. It is a hostile comrade, a domestic enemy.

John Chrysostom

If you would rise, shun luxury, for luxury lowers and degrades.

John Chrysostom

Renunciation of riches is the origin and preserver of virtues.

Ambrose of Milan

Riches are the instrument of all vices, because they render us capable of putting into execution even our worst desires.

Ambrose of Milan

We are born into this world naked, we leave it without a cent, we are buried without our inheritance.

Ambrose of Milan

The earth was made for all, rich and poor, in common. Why do you rich claim it as your exclusive right?

Ambrose of Milan

Opulence is always the result of theft, if not committed by the actual possessor, then by his predecessor.

Jerome

Why would you rejoice in silver? Either your silver will perish, or you will, and no one knows which will perish first. Only one thing is certain: both shall perish.

Augustine of Hippo

All the abundance I have that is not my God is only poverty.

Augustine of Hippo

Don't be anxious about what you have, but about what you are.

Pope Gregory the Great

We should have no more use or regard for money in any of its forms than we have for dust. Those who think it is worth more, or who are greedy for it, expose themselves to the danger of being deceived by the Devil.

Francis of Assisi

How proud we are of gold and silver, which are actually no part of ourselves, but rather are part of the earth—things that are by their nature no better than copper or tin, and much less useful than the poor metal that is used to make the ploughshare, and horseshoes, and horse nails. How proud many men are of those glistening precious stones, of which the very brightest, even if it costs many dollars, will never shine half so bright nor show half so much light as a poor half-penny candle!

Thomas More

Our greatest gain is to lose the wealth that is of such brief duration and, by comparison with eternal things, of such little worth; yet we get upset about it and our gain turns to loss.

Teresa of Avila

Of what use are riches in eternity?

Aloysius Gonzaga

Pharmacists have almost all kinds of poison for their use, as circumstances may require, but they are not poisoned, because they keep their poisons not in their bodies, but in their shops. In like manner you may possess riches without being poisoned by them, provided you have them for use in your house or your purse, and not, by loving them, in your heart.

Francis de Sales

It is not a sin to have riches, but to fix our hearts upon them.

Jean Baptiste de la Salle

If God allows some people to pile up riches instead of making themselves poor as Jesus did, it is so they may use what He has entrusted to them as loyal servants, in accordance with the Master's will, to do spiritual and temporal good to others.

Charles de Foucauld

Don't forget it: He has much who needs least. Don't create necessities for yourself.

Josemaria Escriva

WEATHER

There's no such thing as bad weather. All weather is good because it's God's.

Teresa of Avila

THE WICKED, PROSPERITY OF

When she asked why the wicked often prosper, God said to her:
If I gave temporal goods only to my friends, the wicked would despair and the good would grow proud. Therefore, temporal goods are given to all so that I, the Creator and Giver of all, may be loved by all.

Bridget of Sweden

WISDOM

By what has been, let us avoid what is to be; let us be taught by what has come, to escape what is coming; let us remember what is past, to avoid what is future.

Ephraem the Syrian

Wisdom is the foundation, and justice is the work without which a foundation cannot stand.

Ambrose of Milan

What am I without You, Lord, but a guide to my own downfall?

Augustine of Hippo

Among all human pursuits, the pursuit of wisdom is more perfect, more noble, more useful, and more full of joy.

Thomas Aquinas

What a sacred ignorance it is that loses sight of the wisdom and prudence of this age in order to learn the science and wisdom of the saints in the school of the Holy Spirit!

Paul of the Cross

WOMEN

You, who have the kingdom of heaven, are not a poor little woman, but a queen.

Jordan of Saxony

It is most laudable in a married woman to be devout, but she must never forget that she is a housewife; and sometimes she must leave God at the altar to find Him in her housekeeping.

Frances of Rome

Being a wife and mother was never an obstacle to my spiritual life.

Concepcion Cabrera de Armida

I wish that men were as resolute as women.

Anne Javouhey

In three different ways, woman can fulfill the mission of motherliness: in marriage, in the practice of a profession that values human development ... and under the veil as the spouse of Christ.

Edith Stein

WOMEN, RELIGIOUS — *See Religious Life; Virgins, Consecrated*

WORK

To work is to pray.

Benedict of Nursia

He who labors as he prays lifts his heart to God with his hands.

Benedict of Nursia

All devotion that leads to sloth is false. We must love work.

Zita

Without work, it's impossible to have fun.

Thomas Aquinas

The true apostolic life consists in giving oneself no rest or repose.

Camillus de Lellis

Let us work as if success depends on us alone, but with the heartfelt conviction that we are doing nothing and God everything.

Ignatius Loyola

You must lovingly leave some work to others and not seek to have all the crowns.

Francis de Sales

Let us love God, but with the strength of our arms, in the sweat of our brow.

Vincent de Paul

The chief thing is to take the burden on one's shoulders. As you press forward, it soon shakes down and the load is evenly distributed.

John Bosco

The Servant of Charity must go to bed each night so tired from work that he will think he has been beaten.

Louis Guanella

We will lie down for such a long time after death that it is worthwhile to keep standing while we are alive. Let us work now; one day we shall rest.

Agostina Pietrantoni

Each small task of everyday life is part of the total harmony of the universe.

Thérèse of Lisieux

Only work that is well done and lovingly completed deserves the praise of the Lord.... The fullness of life that God rightly expects from His children means that they have to have a careful concern for the quality of their everyday work, because it is this work, even in its most minor aspects, which they must sanctify.

Josemaria Escriva

If the fact that God sees us were fully impressed on our consciences, and if we realized that all our work, absolutely all of it, is done in His presence—for nothing escapes His eyes—how carefully we would finish things and how differently we would react!

Josemaria Escriva

THE WORLD, WORLDLINESS—
See also Detachment From the World

This world and the world to come are two enemies. We cannot therefore be friends to both; but we must decide which we will forsake and which we will enjoy.

Pope Clement I

What can the world promise? Let it promise you what it will; it is making that promise to someone who may die tomorrow.

Augustine of Hippo

Addressing the world:
Those who love you do not know you; those who despise you, understand you. Thus you are not truthful, but deceitful—you make yourself true, yet show yourself false.

Columbanus

All the ways of the world are as fickle and unstable as a sudden storm at sea.

Bede the Venerable

Worldly people often purchase hell at a very dear price by sacrificing themselves to please the world.

Henry Suso

Let the world indulge its madness, for it cannot endure and passes like a shadow. It is growing old and is, I think, in its last decrepit stage. But we, buried deeply in the wounds of Christ, why should we be dismayed?

Peter Canisius

Who doesn't see that the world is an unjust judge, gracious and favorable to its own children, but harsh and rigorous toward the children of God? We can never please the world unless we lose ourselves together with the world. It's so whimsical that it's impossible to satisfy it.... Whatever we do, the world will wage war against us.

Francis de Sales

The world considers us fools; we must consider it crazy.

Francis de Sales

One single day of devotion is preferable to a thousand years of a worldly life.

Francis de Sales

The spirit of the world is restless and eager to do all things; leave that spirit alone.

Vincent de Paul

When I say "the world," I mean the corrupt and disordered life led in the world, the damnable spirit that reigns over the world, the perverse senti-ments and inclinations that men of the world follow, and the pernicious laws and maxims by which they govern their behavior. Christ looks upon the world as the object of His hatred and His curse, and as something He plans and desires to burn in the day of His wrath.

John Eudes

To his executioners:
My heart is too big for this world, and nothing here can satisfy it.

Theophane Venard

You must either conquer the world or the world will conquer you. You must be either master or slave.

John Henry Cardinal Newman

WORRY
By the anxieties and worries of this life Satan tries to dull man's heart and make a dwelling for himself there.

Francis of Assisi

For pity's sake, don't start meeting troubles halfway.

Teresa of Avila

Anxiety is the greatest evil that can befall the soul, sin only excepted.

Francis de Sales

God commands you to pray, but He forbids you to worry.

John Vianney

I worry until midnight, and from then on I let God worry.

Louis Guanella

WORSHIP— *See also Liturgy*
Men invariably worship what they like best.

Jerome

It is the highest duty of religion to imitate Him whom you adore.

Augustine of Hippo

WRITING

I attempt to be one of those who write because they have made some progress, and who, by means of writing, make further progress.

Augustine of Hippo

Never commit the first line of a book to paper unless you have already written the last word in your mind. Ten years of reading, twenty of meditation, and one of writing, if you want to produce anything worthwhile.

Dominic Barberi

I must not be carried away by the desire to write learnedly and display erudition. If brilliant sayings flash into my mind, I will first ask myself if, at the hour of death, I shall be glad to have said them; and then omit them.

Dominic Barberi

YOUNG PEOPLE, YOUTH

Let us teach the young in the school of the fear of the Lord.

Pope Clement I

Young people especially should fight cheerfully, since Our Lord has so kindly called you in the morning of your days, and not exposed you to the anguish and remorse we feel after so many years of sin.

Elizabeth Ann Seton

Remember that He too was once a young man, for Jesus Christ is the God-Child, the God-Youth, the God-Man, the God of all ages.

Theophane Venard

The soul of youth is ... a most holy sanctuary.

Pope Pius X

ZEAL

Any time is the right time to do with zeal whatever pleases God.

Basil the Great

No sacrifice is more acceptable to God than zeal for souls.

Pope Gregory the Great

Zeal without knowledge is always less useful and effective than regulated zeal, and very often is highly dangerous.

Bernard of Clairvaux

SAINT BIOGRAPHIES

Abba (Abbot) St. Agatho, 4th century, Egyptian; abbot

St. Agnes, d. c. 304, Roman; consecrated virgin and martyr

Blessed Agostina Pietrantoni, 1864–1894, Italian; nun and martyr, nurse

St. Aloysius Gonzaga, 1568–1591, Italian; Jesuit teacher, health care worker

St. Alphonsus Liguori, 1696–1787, Italian; bishop, Doctor of the Church, founder and first superior of the Redemptorists

St. Ambrose of Milan, c. 340–397, German; bishop, Doctor of the Church

St. Ammonas the Hermit, c. 288–350, Egyptian; abbot, associate of St. Antony the Great

Blessed Brother Andre Bessette, 1845–1937, Canadian; brother of the Congregation of the Holy Cross

St. Andrew of Crete, 660–740, Syrian; archbishop, monk, hymnist

Blessed Angela of Foligno, 1248–1309, Italian; hermit, mystic, visionary

St. Angela Merici, c. 1470–1540, Italian; founder and first superior of the Ursulines

Blessed Anna Maria Taigi, 1769–1837, Italian; wife and mother, visionary

Blessed Anne Javouhey, 1798–1851, French; founder of the Congregation of St. Joseph of Cluny, missionary educator

St. Anselm of Canterbury, c. 1033–1109, Italian; archbishop, abbot, theologian, Doctor of the Church

Blessed Anthony Grassi, 1592–1671, Italian; Oratorian superior

St. Anthony Mary Claret, 1807–1870, Spanish; priest, founder of the Missionary Sons of the Immaculate Heart of Mary (Claretians)

St. Anthony Mary Zaccaria, 1502–1539, Italian; priest, reformer, cofounder of the Clerks Regular of St. Paul (Barnabites)

St. Anthony of Padua, 1195–1231, Portuguese; Franciscan preacher and reformer, Doctor of the Church

St. Antony the Great, 251–356, Egyptian; abbot, "Father of Christian Monasticism"

St. Arsenius the Great, c. 355–c. 450, Roman; deacon, monk

St. Athanasius of Alexandria, c. 297–373, Egyptian; bishop, theologian, Doctor of the Church

St. Augustine of Hippo, 354–430, north African; bishop, theologian, Doctor of the Church

St. Avitus of Vienna, d. c. 519, Gallic; bishop, poet

St. Barsanuphius, 6th century, Egyptian; hermit

St. Basil the Great, 329–379; Cappadocian; bishop, theologian, monk

St. Bede the Venerable, c. 673–735, English; priest, monk, scholar, Doctor of the Church

St. Benedict Joseph Labre, 1748–1783, French; pilgrim and mendicant

St. Benedict of Nursia, c. 480–c. 547, Italian; abbot, "Father of Western Monasticism"

St. Benildus, 1805–1862, French; Christian Brothers teacher

St. Bernadette Soubirous, 1844–1879, French; visionary of Marian apparitions at Lourdes

St. Bernard of Clairvaux, 1090–1153, French; abbot, mystical writer, theologian, reformer of the Cistercian Order, Doctor of the Church

St. Bernardino of Siena, 1380–1444, Italian; priest, Franciscan vicar general, preacher, reformer

Blessed Queen Blanche of France, d. 1253, Spanish; wife and mother, queen of France; mother and regent of King St. Louis IX

St. Bonaventure, 1221–1274, Italian; cardinal–bishop, Franciscan minister general, philosopher, theologian, Doctor of the Church

St. Boniface of Mainz, 974–1009, German; missionary archbishop, monk

St. Bridget of Sweden, 1303–1373, Swedish; wife and mother, mystical writer, visionary, reformer, founder of the Order of the Most Holy Trinity (Brigettines)

St. Bruno Serunkuma of Uganda, d. 1886, Ugandan; martyr

St. Caesarius of Arles, 470–543, Gallic; archbishop, monk

St. Camillus de Lellis, 1550–1614, Neapolitan; priest, founder and first superior–general of the Ministers of the Sick (Camellians)

St. Catherine of Genoa, 1447–1510, Italian; wife, mystical writer, visionary, hospital director

St. Catherine Laboure, 1806–1876, French; Sister of Charity of St. Vincent de Paul; visionary responsible for the creation of the Miraculous Medal

St. Catherine of Siena, 1347–1380, Italian; Dominican tertiary, mystical writer, visionary, Doctor of the Church

Blessed Charles of Blois, d. 1364, French; husband and father, duke, soldier

St. Charles Cardinal Borromeo, 1538–1584, Italian; cardinal archbishop, reformer, founder of the Oblates of St. Ambrose (now Oblates of St. Charles)

Venerable Charles de Foucauld, 1858–1916, French; priest, hermit, explorer

St. Charles of Sezze, 1616–1670, Italian; lay brother, mystical writer, health care worker

St. Chromatius of Aquileia, d. c. 407, Italian; bishop, scholar

St. Clare of Assisi, 1194–1253, Italian; founder and first superior of the Franciscan Poor Clares

St. Claude de la Colombiere, 1641–1682, French; Jesuit priest, superior, missionary, ascetical writer

Pope St. Clement I, d. c. 99, Roman; pope, martyr

St. Clement of Alexandria, c. 150–c. 215, Greek; theologian, head of the Catechetical School at Alexandria, Egypt

St. Clotilda, 474–545, French; wife and mother, queen of the Franks

St. Columbanus, 540–615, Irish; monk, missionary

Venerable Servant of God Concepcion Cabrera de Armida, 1862–1937, Mexican; wife and mother, instrumental in the founding of the five "Works of the Cross."

St. Crispina of Thacora, d. 304, north African; wife and mother, martyr

St. Cyprian of Carthage, c. 200–258, north African; bishop; biblical scholar, martyr

St. Cyril of Alexandria, c. 376–444, Egyptian; bishop, theologian, Doctor of the Church

St. Cyril of Jerusalem, c. 315–386, Palestinian; bishop, scholar, Doctor of the Church

St. Dominic, 1170–1221, Spanish; priest, preacher, founder of the Order of Preachers (Dominicans)

Blessed Dominic Barberi, 1792–1849, Italian; Passionist priest and missionary, theologian, mystical writer

St. Dominic Savio, 1842–1857, Italian; child visionary, founder of the Company of the Immaculate Conception

St. Dorotheos of Gaza, c. 506–560, Syrian; abbot, ascetical writer

St. Edith Stein, 1891–1942, German; Carmelite nun, philosopher, martyr

St. Edmund of Abingdon, c. 1180–1240, English; archbishop

St. Elizabeth Ann Seton, 1774–1821, American; wife and mother, founder and first superior of the Sisters of Charity

St. Elizabeth of Hungary, 1207–1231, Hungarian; wife and mother, Franciscan tertiary, health care worker

St. Ephraem the Syrian, c. 306–373, Syrian; deacon, hymnist, poet

St. Epiphanius of Salamis, c. 315–403, Palestinian; bishop, abbot, scholar

Blessed Eugenie Smet, 1825–1871, French; founder of the Helpers of the Holy Souls

St. Eusebius of Vercelli, c. 283–371, Sardinian; bishop

St. Febronia, d. c. 304, Syrian; consecrated virgin, martyr

St. Fidelis of Sigmaringen, 1577–1622, German; Capuchin priest, missionary, martyr

St. Frances of Rome, 1384–1440, Italian; wife and mother, visionary, founder and superior of the Oblates of Mary

St. Frances Xavier Cabrini, 1850–1917, Italian; missionary, educator, founder of the Missionary Sisters of the Sacred Heart

St. Francis of Assisi, c. 1181–1226, Italian; preacher, mystic, stigmatist, founder of the Order of Friars Minor (Franciscans)

Blessed Francis Libermann, 1804–1852, French; priest, missionary, founder of the Holy Ghost Fathers

St. Francis of Paola, c. 1416–1507, Italian; hermit, founder of the Minim Friars

St. Francis de Sales, 1567–1622, French; bishop, missionary, cofounder of the Order of the Visitation (Visitandines), Doctor of the Church

St. Francis Xavier, 1506–1552, Spanish; Jesuit priest and missionary

St. Fulgence of Ruspe, 467–527, north African; bishop, monk, theologian

St. Gabriel Possenti, 1838–1862, Italian; Passionist priest

St. Gemma Galgani, 1878–1903, Italian; visionary, stigmatist

St. Gertrude the Great, c. 1256–c.1302, German; Benedictine nun, visionary, spiritual writer

Pope St. Gregory I (the Great), c. 540–604, Roman; pope, abbot, liturgist, reformer, statesman, Doctor of the Church

Pope St. Gregory VII, c. 1021–1085, Italian; pope, reformer

St. Gregory of Elvira, d. after 392, Spanish; bishop, theologian

St. Gregory Nazianzen, c. 329–389, Cappadocian; archbishop, theologian, Doctor of the Church

St. Gregory of Nyssa, c. 330–c. 395, Cappadocian; bishop, theologian

St. Hedwig of Silesia, c. 1174–1243, German; wife and mother, duchess, founder of monasteries and hospitals

St. Henry Morse, 1595–1645, English; Jesuit priest, missionary, martyr

Blessed Henry Suso, c. 1295–1365, Swiss; Dominican priest, prior, visionary, mystical writer

Blessed Herman of Reichenau, 1013–1054, German; monk, mathematician, historian, hymnist, poet

St. Herve of Brittany, d. c. 575, French; abbot, schoolmaster, hymnist

St. Hilarion, c. 291–371, Palestinian; hermit

St. Hilary of Poitiers, d. c. 368, Gallic; husband, bishop, theologian, Doctor of the Church

St. Hildegard of Bingen, 1098–1179, German; prioress, founder of convents, visionary, spiritual writer

St. Ignatius of Antioch, d. c. 107, Syrian; bishop, martyr

St. Ignatius Loyola, 1491–1556, Spanish; priest, spiritual writer, founder and first superior general of the Society of Jesus (Jesuits)

St. Irenaeus of Lyons, c. 125–c. 203, Asia Minor; bishop, missionary, theologian, defender of orthodoxy

St. Isidore of Seville, c. 560–636, Spanish; bishop, scholar, educator, liturgist, philosopher, Doctor of the Church

Blessed Jan Van Ruysbroeck, 1293–1381, Flemish; priest, prior, mystical writer

St. Jane Frances de Chantal, 1572–1641, French; wife and mother, cofounder of the Congregation of the Visitation (Visitandines)

St. Jean Baptiste de la Salle, 1651–1719, French; priest, educator, founder of the Institute of the Brothers of the Christian Schools

St. Jerome, c. 342–420, Dalmatian; priest, hermit, abbot, biblical scholar and translator, Doctor of the Church

St. Jerome Emiliani, 1481–1537, Italian; priest, soldier, founder of orphanages and other charitable works, founder of the Clerks Regular of Somascha

St. John of Avila, 1499–1569, Spanish; priest, preacher, missionary, spiritual director

St. John Bosco, 1815–1888, Italian; priest, educator, founder of the Society of St. Francis de Sales (Salesians) and the Daughters of Our Lady, Help of Christians

St. John Chrysostom, c. 347–407, Syrian; archbishop, Doctor of the Church

St. John Climacus, c. 569–c. 649, Syrian; abbot, ascetical writer

St. John of the Cross, 1542–1591, Spanish; Carmelite priest, provincial, reformer, mystical writer, Doctor of the Church

St. John of Damascus, c. 675–c. 749, Syrian; priest, monk, theologian, poet, Doctor of the Church

St. John Eudes, 1601–1680, French; priest, missionary, founder of seminaries and of the Congregation of Jesus and Mary (Eudists)

St. John of God, 1495–1550, Portuguese; founder of the Order of Brothers Hospitalers

Venerable John Henry Cardinal Newman, 1801–1890, English; cardinal, theologian, apologist

St. John the Short, 5th century, Egyptian; monk

St. John Vianney, 1786–1859, French; priest, spiritual director

Blessed Jordan of Saxony, d. 1237, German; succeeded St. Dominic as second Master of the Order of Preachers (Dominicans)

Blessed Josemaria Escriva, 1902–1975, Spanish; priest, founder of Opus Dei and the Priestly Society of the Holy Cross

St. Joseph Cafasso, 1811–1860, Italian; priest, spiritual director

St. Joseph of Calasanza, 1556–1648, Spanish; priest, educator, founder of the Clerks Regular of Religious Schools (Piarists)

St. Joseph of Cupertino, 1603–1663, Italian; priest, Franciscan tertiary

St. Joseph Mukasa Balikuddembe, d. 1885, Ugandan; chief steward of the king, martyr

Blessed Julian of Norwich, c. 1342–1423, English; hermit, visionary, mystical writer

Blessed Juniperro Serra, 1713–1784, Majorcan; Franciscan priest, missionary, university professor

St. Justin Martyr, c. 100–c. 165, Samaritan; philosopher, apologist, martyr

St. Lawrence of Brindisi, 1559–1619, Neapolitan; priest, vicar general of the Capuchins, missionary, army chaplain, Doctor of the Church

Pope St. Leo I (the Great), d. 461, Roman; pope, Doctor of the Church

St. Leonard of Port Maurice, 1676–1751, Italian; Franciscan priest, missionary

King St. Louis IX of France, 1214–1270, French; husband and father, king of France

Blessed Louis Guanella, 1842–1915, Italian; founder of the Servants of Charity, homes for the mentally disabled

St. Louis de Montfort, 1673–1716, French; priest, missionary, spiritual writer, founder of the Daughters of Divine Wisdom and the Missionaries of the Company of Mary

St. Lucy, d. 304, Sicilian; consecrated virgin, martyr

St. Macra, d. c. 297, Gallic; consecrated virgin, martyr

St. Madeleine Sophie Barat, 1779–1865, French; superior of the Society of the Sacred Heart of Jesus

St. Margaret of Cortona, 1247–1297, Italian; visionary, Franciscan tertiary, founder of the Confraternity of Our Lady of Mercy

St. Margaret Mary Alacoque, 1647–1690, French; Visitandine visionary, promoter of devotion to the Sacred Heart of Jesus

St. Margaret of Youville, 1701–1771, Canadian; wife and mother, founder of the Sisters of Charity (Gray Nuns)

Blessed Maria Droste zu Vischering, 1863–1899, German; superior in the Order of the Good Shepherd

St. Maria Goretti, 1890–1902, Italian; murdered for resisting an attempted rape; she forgave her murderer before she died, and he was converted in prison

Blessed Mariam Baouardy, 1846–1878, Palestinian; Carmelite missionary

Blessed Marie of the Incarnation, 1599–1672, French; wife and mother, Ursuline missionary and educator, mystical writer

St. Mark the Ascetic, 5th century, Byzantine; hermit, abbot, ascetical writer

St. Martin of Tours, c. 316–c. 397, Hungarian; bishop, monk, missionary, pioneer of Western monasticism

Venerable Mary Magdalen Bentivoglio, 1834–1905, Italian; founded the first Poor Clares in the U.S.

St. Mary Magdalene dei Pazzi, 1566–1607, Italian; Carmelite visionary and mystic

St. Mary Mazzarello, 1837–1881, Italian; first superior of the Daughters of Our Lady, Help of Christians (Salesian Sisters)

St. Maximillian Kolbe, 1894–1941, Polish; Franciscan priest, founder of Knights of Mary Immaculate, martyr

St. Maximus the Confessor, c. 580–662, Byzantine; abbot, confessor, theologian, mystical and ascetical writer

St. Miguel of Ecuador, 1857–1910, Ecuadoran; Christian Brother, educator

St. Monica, c. 331–387, north African; wife and mother; mother of St. Augustine of Hippo

St. Moses the Black, c. 330–c. 405, Ethiopian; priest, monk

St. Niceta of Remesiana, c. 335–c. 414, Dacian?; bishop, missionary, hymnist, spiritual writer

St. Nicholas of Flue, 1417–1487, Swiss; husband and father, hermit

St. Pacianus of Barcelona, 4th century, Spanish; husband and father, bishop

St. Patrick of Ireland, c. 389–c. 461, British or perhaps Gallic; bishop, missionary, "apostle of the Irish"

St. Paul of the Cross, 1694–1775, Italian; monk, preacher, visionary, founder and first superior general of the Barefoot Clerks of the Holy Cross and Passion (Passionists)

St. Paulinus of Nola, c. 354–431, Gallic; husband and father, bishop, poet

St. Peter of Alcantara, 1499–1562, Spanish; Franciscan minister provincial, reformer, founder of the Franciscans of the Observance of St. Peter of Alcantara (Alcantarines)

St. Peter Canisius, 1521–1597, Dutch; Jesuit priest, scholar and educator; founder of colleges, Doctor of the Church

St. Peter Chrysologus, 406–c. 450, Italian; bishop, Doctor of the Church

St. Peter Claver, 1580–1654, Spanish; Jesuit priest, missionary to slaves

St. Peter Damian, 1001–1072, Italian; cardinal–bishop, Benedictine prior, spiritual writer, Doctor of the Church

St. Peter Julian Eymard, 1811–1868, French; Marist priest and provincial; founder of Priests of the Blessed Sacrament and Servants of the Blessed Sacrament

St. Philip Neri, 1515–1595, Italian; priest, preacher, visionary, founder and first superior of the Oratorians

Blessed Padre Pio of Pietrelcina, 1887–1968, Italian; Capuchin priest, visionary, mystic, stigmatist

St. Pior, 4th century, Egyptian; hermit

Pope St. Pius X, 1835–1914, Italian; pope, reformer

Blessed Placid Riccardi, 1844–1915, Italian; Benedictine priest

Abba (Abbot) St. Poemen, 4th or 5th century, Egyptian; monk, ascetical and mystical writer

St. Polycarp of Smyrna, c. 69–c. 165, Asia Minor; bishop, defender of orthodoxy, martyr

Blessed Raphaela Maria Porras, 1850–1925, Spanish; cofounder and first mother general of the Handmaids of the Sacred Heart

St. Richard of Chichester, c. 1197–1254, English; bishop, doctor of canon law, university chancellor

Blessed Richard Rolle, c. 1300–1349, English; hermit, mystical writer

St. Robert Cardinal Bellarmine, 1542–1621, Italian; cardinal-archbishop, Jesuit provincial, theologian, university professor, scholar, apologist, Doctor of the Church

St. Robert Southwell, c. 1561–1595, English; Jesuit priest, missionary, martyr, poet

St. Romuald, c. 950–1027, Italian; Benedictine abbot, founder of the Camaldolese Order

St. Rose of Lima, 1586–1617, Peruvian; consecrated virgin, Dominican tertiary, visionary

St. Sebastian Valfre, 1629–1710, Italian; Oratorian priest, preacher

St. Serapion, d. c. 370, Egyptian; monk

St. Severinus (Boethius), c. 480–c. 524, Roman; philosopher, statesman, martyr

St. Simeon the Insane, d. c. 589, Egyptian; hermit

St. Sisois, 4th century, Egyptian; hermit

Pope St. Stephen I, d. 257, Roman; pope

Amma (Abbess) St. Syncletice, 4th century, Egyptian; abbess

St. Teresa of Avila, 1515–1582, Spanish; Carmelite reformer, mystical writer, Doctor of the Church

St. Theonas, 4th century, Egyptian; hermit

St. Theophane Venard, 1829–1861, French; priest, missionary, martyr

St. Theophilus of Antioch, d. c. 185, Syrian; bishop, theologian, apologist

St. Thérèse of Lisieux, 1873–1897, French; Carmelite mystic, Doctor of the Church

St. Thomas Aquinas, c. 1225–1274, Italian; Dominican philosopher, theologian, mystic, hymnist, Doctor of the Church

St. Thomas More, 1478–1535, English; husband and father, scholar, statesman, lawyer, spiritual writer, martyr

St. Thomas of Villanova, 1488–1555, Spanish; archbishop, Augustinian provincial, university professor, reformer, chaplain to the emperor

St. Venantius of Camerino, d. c. 250, Roman; martyr

St. Venantius Fortunatus, c. 530–c. 610, Italian; bishop, poet, hymnist

St. Vincent Ferrer, 1350–1419, Spanish; Dominican priest, missionary

St. Vincent of Lerins, d. before 450, Gallic; monk, theologian

St. Vincent Pallotti, 1795–1850, Italian; priest, missionary, exorcist, founder of the Society of the Catholic Apostolate

St. Vincent de Paul, c. 1580–1660, French; priest, missionary, founder of the Congregation of the Mission (Vincentians and Lazarists); cofounder of the Sisters of Charity

St. Zita, 1218–c. 1272, Italian; consecrated virgin, household servant